HOW IT WORKS

FLIGHT

BILL GUNSTON

award

Series editor: Elizabeth Miles
Cover design: Duck Egg Blue
Illustrations: Ian Howatson and Sebastian Quigley
Photographs: AeroVironment, Inc., Arpingstone, Lance Cpl Tyler Harmon, NASA, NASA/Carla Thomas, San Diego Air & Space Museum, Shutterstock.com (1989studio, desertfox99, Everett Collection, Felix Marx, Gary L. Brewer, Iakov Filimonov, James Arup, Jeff Schultes, KITTIPHONG PHONGAEN, Kletr, Konwicki Marcin, Martijn Smeets, Mikado767, Mikhail Starodubov, Newcastle, Peter Baxter, ra.photo, ranchorunner, Skycolors, Soonthorn Wongsaita, topseller, twintyre, Vargadosareka)

ISBN 978-1-78270-002-9

This edition first published 2026

Published by Award Publications Limited,
The Old Riding School, Welbeck, Worksop, S80 3LR

 awardpublications @award.books
www.awardpublications.co.uk

26-1217 1

Printed in China

Contents

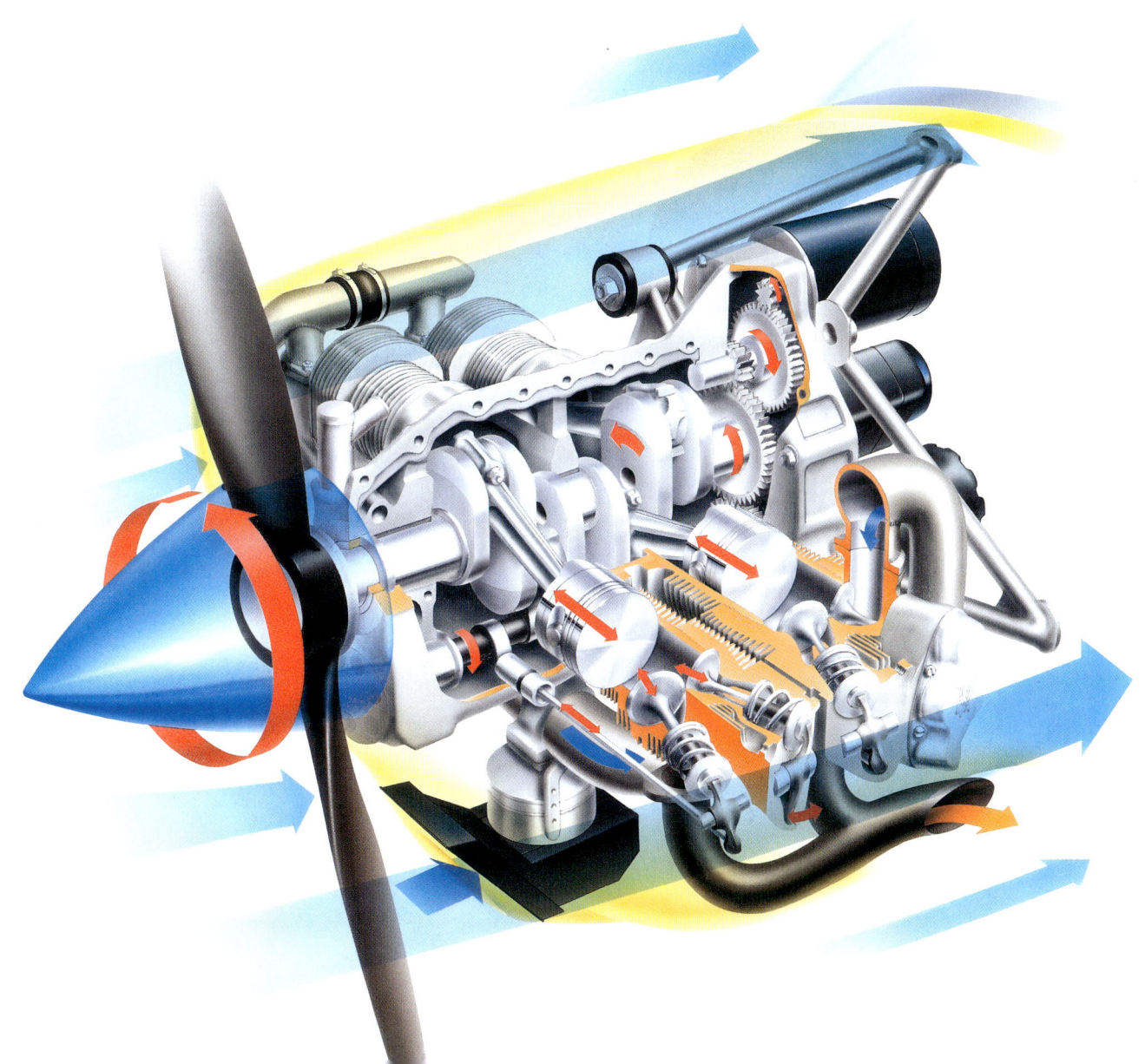

Balloons

Over 240 years ago, in 1783, two Frenchmen, Joseph and Etienne Montgolfier, invented the first hot air balloon. Although they did not realise it themselves, their design worked because hot air rises as it is less dense than cold air. The hot, lower-density air inside a hot air balloon makes the balloon lighter than the cooler, higher-density air around it, which forces the balloon to rise.

Today, many people enjoy ballooning as a leisure activity. Balloonists are carried in a strong, but light, basket suspended beneath the balloon. The basket also holds tanks of liquid fuel, called propane, which feed a burner. The burner sends a long flame into the balloon to heat the air inside, gently lifting it to flying altitude. The balloon then floats along in the air, carried by the wind. From time to time, the air inside has to be heated up again by turning on the burner. If the balloon's air is not reheated, the balloon will begin to descend.

Montgolfier

Balloon made of canvas covered with paper

Brazier

In 1783, the Montgolfier balloon (*above*) carried the first people on an air flight of any kind. Cords supported the wickerwork gallery at the bottom and chains held the brazier under the envelope. The Montgolfier brothers did not know it was the hot air from the burning straw and wool in the brazier that made it fly; they thought that the fire produced a special gas that made the balloon rise.

Hydrogen balloon

The same year that the Montgolfier brothers made their pioneering flight (*above right*), Jacques Charles and Nicolas-Louis Robert were experimenting with the first balloons to be filled with a low-density gas in place of hot air. Hydrogen is the lightest of all gases, so it gives the most powerful lift. Unlike a hot air balloon, a hydrogen balloon does not need a burner.

When the aeronaut (pilot) pulls on a handle, fuel is fed to the burner, producing a jet of flame

The basket is made of strong woven wicker or rattan

Handholds are used to steady the balloon before liftoff and when landing

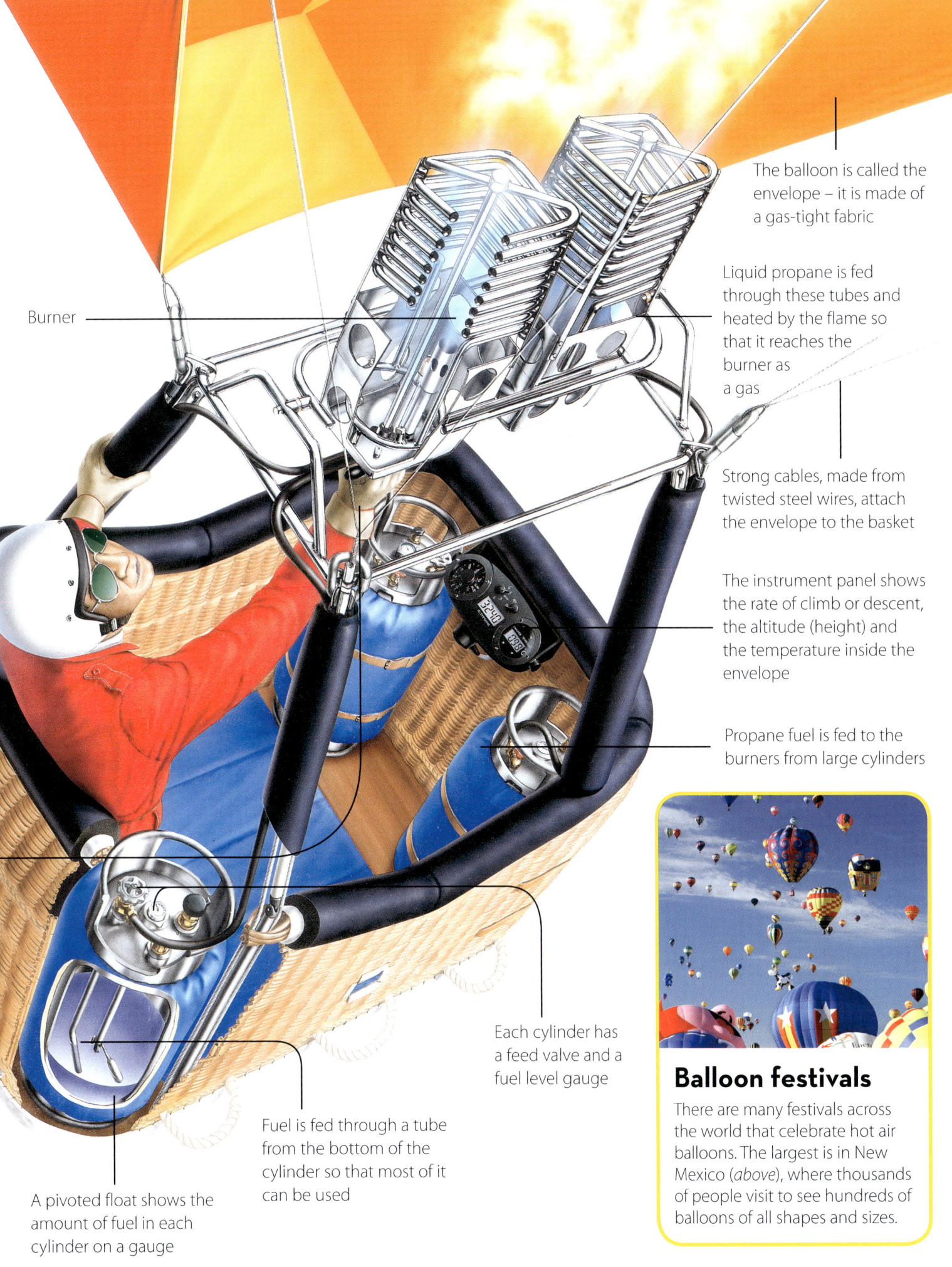

Burner

The balloon is called the envelope – it is made of a gas-tight fabric

Liquid propane is fed through these tubes and heated by the flame so that it reaches the burner as a gas

Strong cables, made from twisted steel wires, attach the envelope to the basket

The instrument panel shows the rate of climb or descent, the altitude (height) and the temperature inside the envelope

Propane fuel is fed to the burners from large cylinders

Each cylinder has a feed valve and a fuel level gauge

Fuel is fed through a tube from the bottom of the cylinder so that most of it can be used

A pivoted float shows the amount of fuel in each cylinder on a gauge

Balloon festivals

There are many festivals across the world that celebrate hot air balloons. The largest is in New Mexico (*above*), where thousands of people visit to see hundreds of balloons of all shapes and sizes.

Airships

Hot air balloons are blown wherever the wind takes them. Airships were invented so that the direction of travel could be controlled. Early airships consisted of an envelope with a rigid frame that contained separate gas bags. Today, airships are non-rigids, or 'blimps', which means they have an envelope made of flexible fabric, like a balloon. Helium gas fills most of the envelope. Helium is less dense, and therefore lighter, than air, so it lifts the airship. The gondola, or cabin, of this non-rigid airship (*right*) carries two piston engines, which drive propellers inside ducts. The ducts can be rotated to make the propellers push the airship forward, up or down.

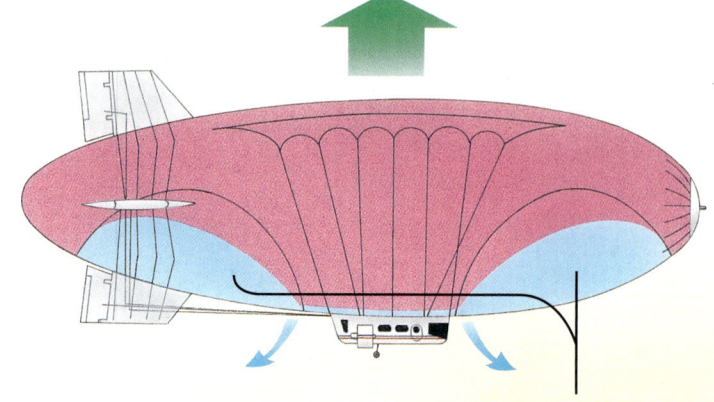

Air bags, called ballonets, lie at the front and back of the airship

Modern airships

Most of the envelope contains helium, which lifts the weight of the airship. But two large bags, called ballonets, contain air. For the airship to rise or fall, air is pumped out of (*above*), or into (*above right*) the ballonets.

These flap valves control the airflow to the rear ballonet

LZ 129 Hindenburg

The *Hindenburg* (*above*) was the largest flying machine ever built. First flown in 1936, it was a rigid hydrogen-filled airship and had 25 double bedrooms for its passengers. In 1937, it was destroyed by fire (*below*) as it attempted to dock.

This tube feeds air to the rear ballonet

The access door to the engine room

This pulley controls the rudders that allow the pilot to steer the airship

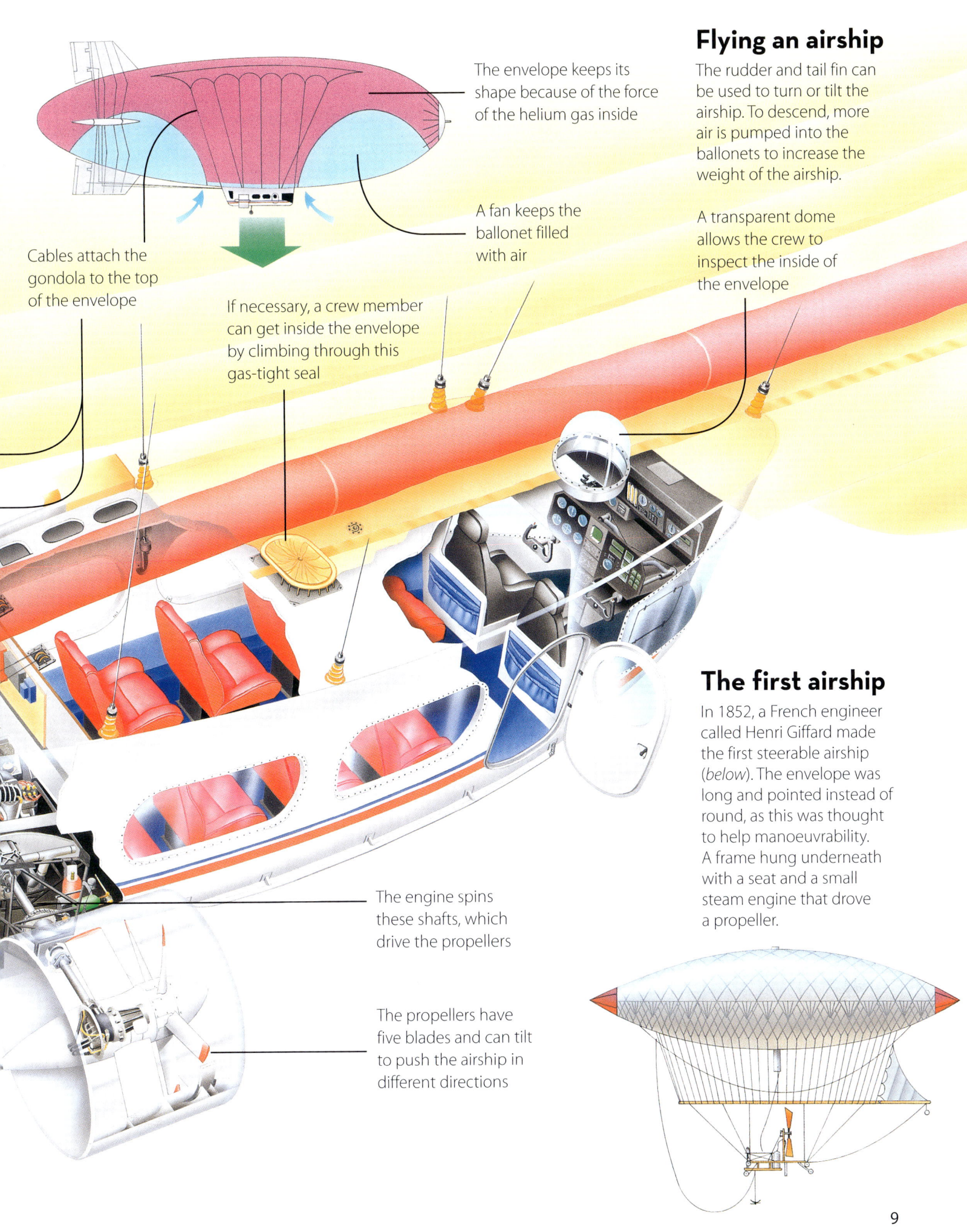

The envelope keeps its shape because of the force of the helium gas inside

A fan keeps the ballonet filled with air

Cables attach the gondola to the top of the envelope

If necessary, a crew member can get inside the envelope by climbing through this gas-tight seal

The engine spins these shafts, which drive the propellers

The propellers have five blades and can tilt to push the airship in different directions

Flying an airship

The rudder and tail fin can be used to turn or tilt the airship. To descend, more air is pumped into the ballonets to increase the weight of the airship.

A transparent dome allows the crew to inspect the inside of the envelope

The first airship

In 1852, a French engineer called Henri Giffard made the first steerable airship (*below*). The envelope was long and pointed instead of round, as this was thought to help manoeuvrability. A frame hung underneath with a seat and a small steam engine that drove a propeller.

9

The First Aeroplane

The first successful powered aeroplane, the *Wright Flyer*, was built by American brothers Wilbur and Orville Wright. They began building gliders in the late 1890s. They spent many hours watching birds, noting the way they flew, and tried to apply these principles in their designs. The brothers' gliders were biplanes, with two sets of wings. As their designs developed, horizontal elevators were added at the front to allow the glider to climb and dive. For steering, two rudders were put in the vertical tail at the back and wires were attached to the wings so they could be warped (or twisted) to make the aircraft roll to the left or right. Finally, a 12-horsepower engine was added to drive two big 'pusher' propellers using bicycle chains. The pilot controlled the elevators with two levers and shifted his body to the left or right in a cradle to pull on the wires attached to the wings and rudders.

Wilbur Wright

Orville Wright

The two rudders were designed to pivot whenever the wings were twisted and were used to steer the aircraft

'Pusher' propellers lie behind the engine, as here, instead of in front – they pushed the *Wright Flyer* along

The upper and lower wings were joined by nine pairs of strong struts and held firm by wires

The aeroplane's framework was made of wood, mostly spruce

The Wrights knew that aircraft wings had to be curved rather than flat

Both wings were covered in muslin fabric

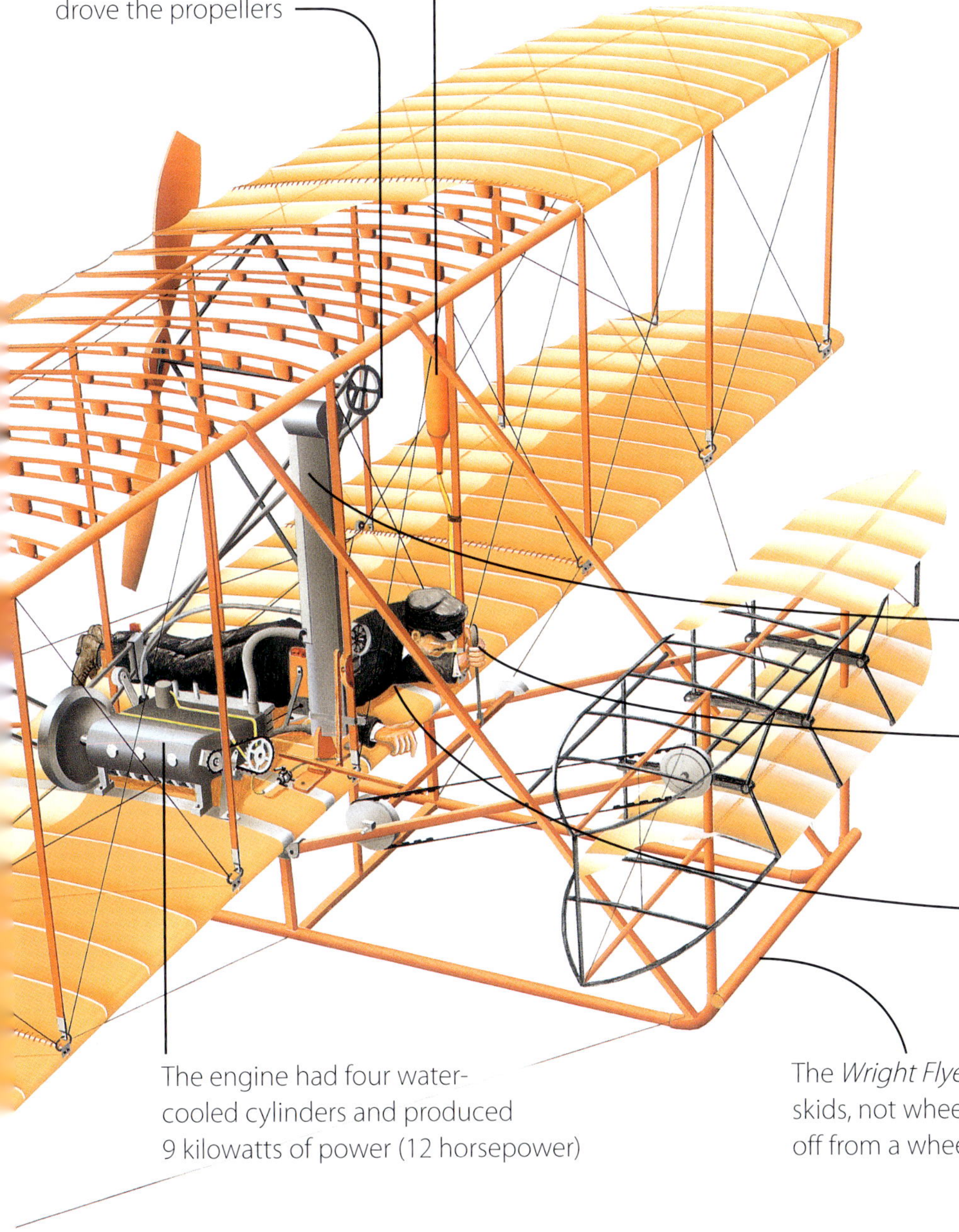

Bicycle chains inside tubes drove the propellers

A petrol tank held fuel for the engines

First flights

Orville Wright made the world's first powered aeroplane flight on 17 December 1903. The photograph above shows him flying the brothers' second aircraft, Wright Flyer II, over Huffman Prairie on November 16, 1904.

The engine water was cooled in this radiator

A control stick moved the front elevators

The pilot lay in a hip cradle that was free to slide to the left or right. By shifting their body weight, the pilot pulled the wires that twisted the wings

The engine had four water-cooled cylinders and produced 9 kilowatts of power (12 horsepower)

The *Wright Flyer* landed on skids, not wheels – it took off from a wheeled trolley

Beech Starship

After the Wright brothers' aeroplane, few aircraft designers put a smaller horizontal forewing, or canard, at the front. It was 70 years before canard aeroplanes came back into fashion. Some recent jet fighters have canards, and even a few business and private aircraft have tested the canard design. The unusual-looking Beech Starship (*right*) first flew in 1986. It was a canard business aircraft, with twin 'pusher' turboprop engines and up to nine seats. Only 53 Starships were ever built.

Early Aeroplanes

Before 1930, most aeroplanes were made of wood, or steel tubes, or both. They were usually kept rigid with tensioned wires and covered with flimsy fabric. Designers then began to make aeroplanes entirely out of metal. A strong metal skin, or outer layer, could withstand the pushing, pulling and twisting forces of flight. This meant that designers could do away with wires and struts. Next, retractable landing gear was added, so the wheels could be folded away inside the aeroplane after takeoff.

Jet aeroplane

First flown on 27 August 1939, the Heinkel He 178 was the first jet aeroplane in the world. It was powered by a turbojet engine invented by German engineer, Hans von Ohain. An Englishman, Frank Whittle, had patented a design for the same kind of engine nine years earlier, but few people believed that it would work.

Swept wings

Engineers discovered that a fast jet can go even faster if its wings are swept back. The Bell X-5 was first flown in America in 1951. Its wings could be pivoted from 20 to 60 degrees during flight.

All-metal aircraft

Apart from an unsuccessful machine in 1910, the Junkers J 1 of December 1915 was the first all-metal aircraft. This German monoplane was made using steel sheets, protected by a thin layer of tin.

Junkers J 1

Heinkel He 178

Bell X-5

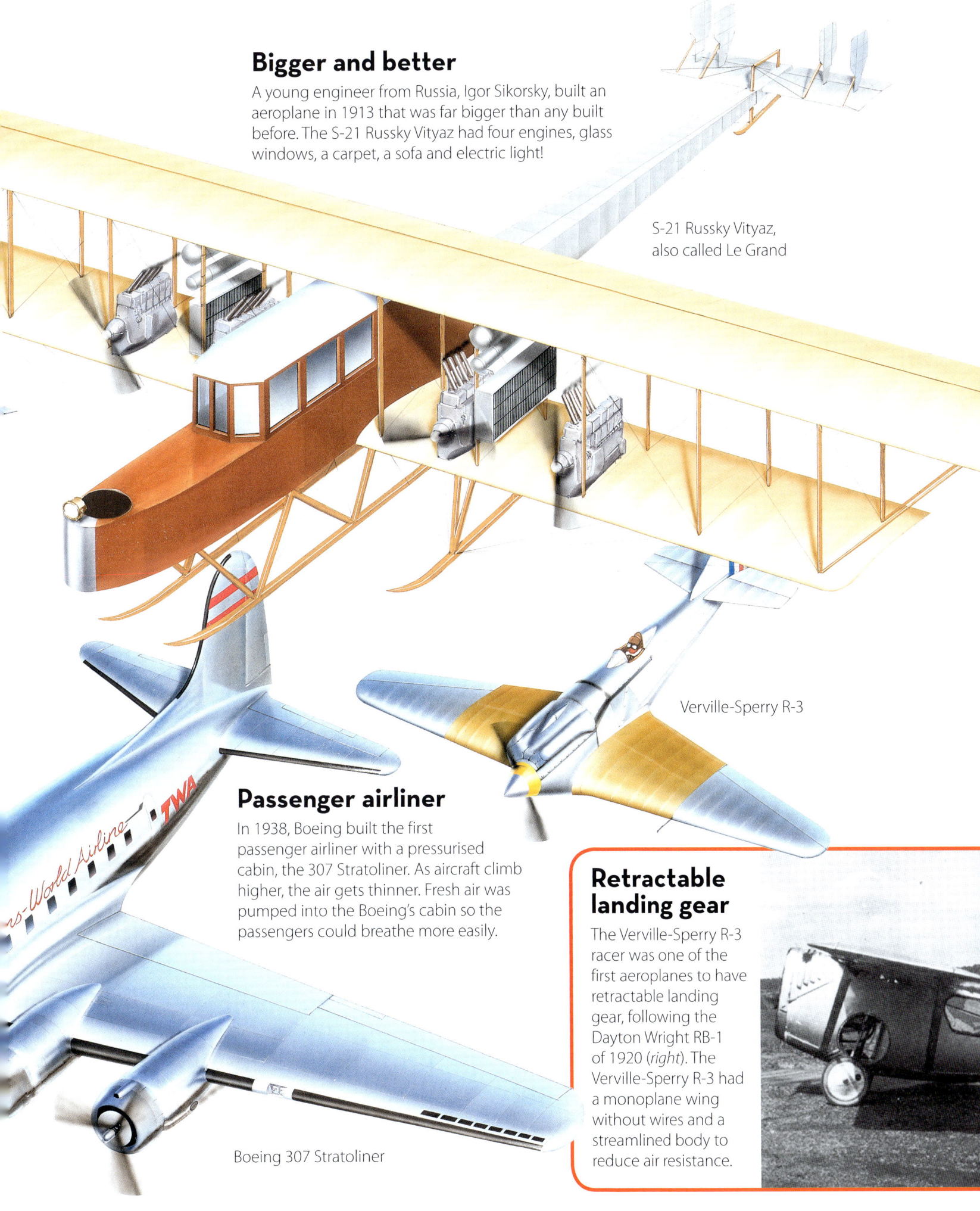

Bigger and better

A young engineer from Russia, Igor Sikorsky, built an aeroplane in 1913 that was far bigger than any built before. The S-21 Russky Vityaz had four engines, glass windows, a carpet, a sofa and electric light!

S-21 Russky Vityaz, also called Le Grand

Verville-Sperry R-3

Passenger airliner

In 1938, Boeing built the first passenger airliner with a pressurised cabin, the 307 Stratoliner. As aircraft climb higher, the air gets thinner. Fresh air was pumped into the Boeing's cabin so the passengers could breathe more easily.

Retractable landing gear

The Verville-Sperry R-3 racer was one of the first aeroplanes to have retractable landing gear, following the Dayton Wright RB-1 of 1920 (*right*). The Verville-Sperry R-3 had a monoplane wing without wires and a streamlined body to reduce air resistance.

Boeing 307 Stratoliner

13

How Aeroplanes Fly

For an aeroplane to fly, it must have one or more wings, a propulsion system (propeller or jet) and flight controls to guide it. To stop an aeroplane from being pulled down to earth by its own weight, a force called lift must be generated. To do this, an aeroplane must be travelling fast enough and its wings must be a special cambered, or curved, shape (*see right*).

The whole body of an aeroplane must have a streamlined, or smooth, shape so air can pass freely around it. A shape that is not streamlined would cause greater friction with the air, known as drag, which works against the aircraft's forward motion.

Lift

The upward force caused by a wing moving through the air is called lift. Almost all lift is produced by the air that passes across the more-curved top of the wing. This air has to speed up and rush over the wing much faster than the air passing underneath. Speeding up the air greatly reduces its pressure, so it sucks the wing upwards.

The fin is like the feathers on a dart or arrow – it keeps the aircraft pointing the right way

Friction with the air causes drag, which acts against the aircraft's forward motion

The tailplane produces forces to help keep the aircraft balanced

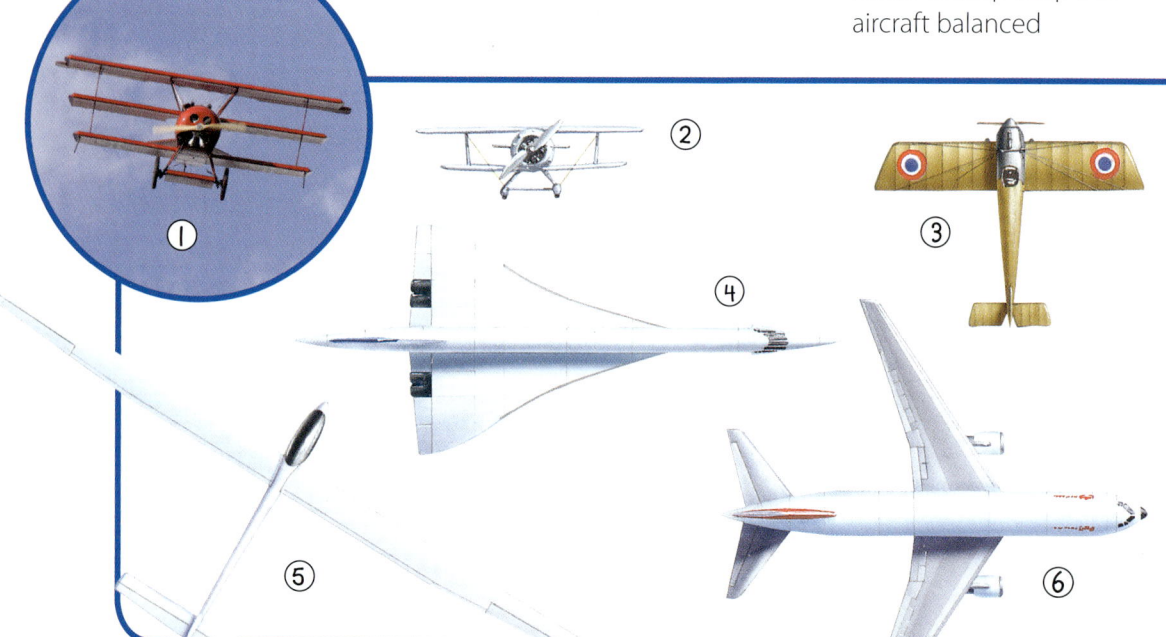

Aeroplane shapes

(1) A triplane (with three sets of wings) fighter of 1917. (2) A biplane (with two sets of wings). (3) A monoplane (with one set of wings) fighter of 1915. (4) The distinctive Concorde, a former supersonic airliner. (5) A glider, with long, slender wings to help it stay airborne without an engine. (6) A passenger airliner with two jet engines.

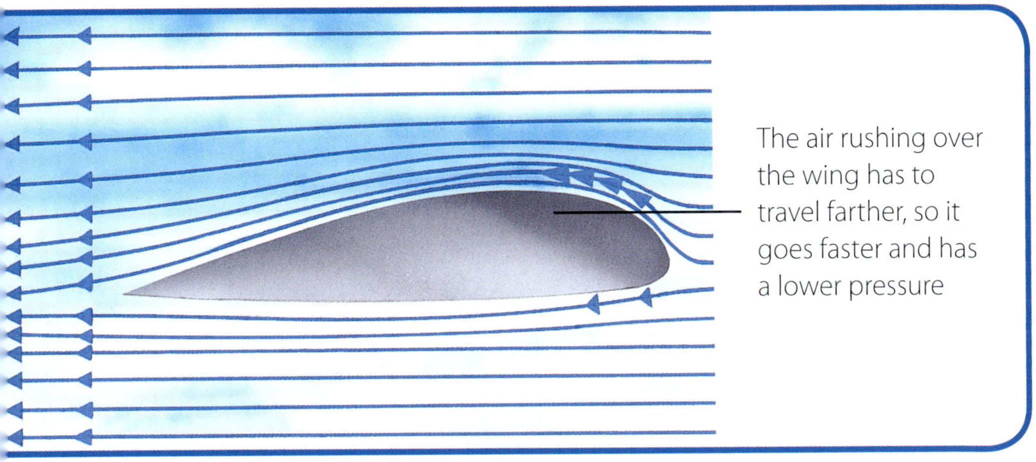

The air rushing over the wing has to travel farther, so it goes faster and has a lower pressure

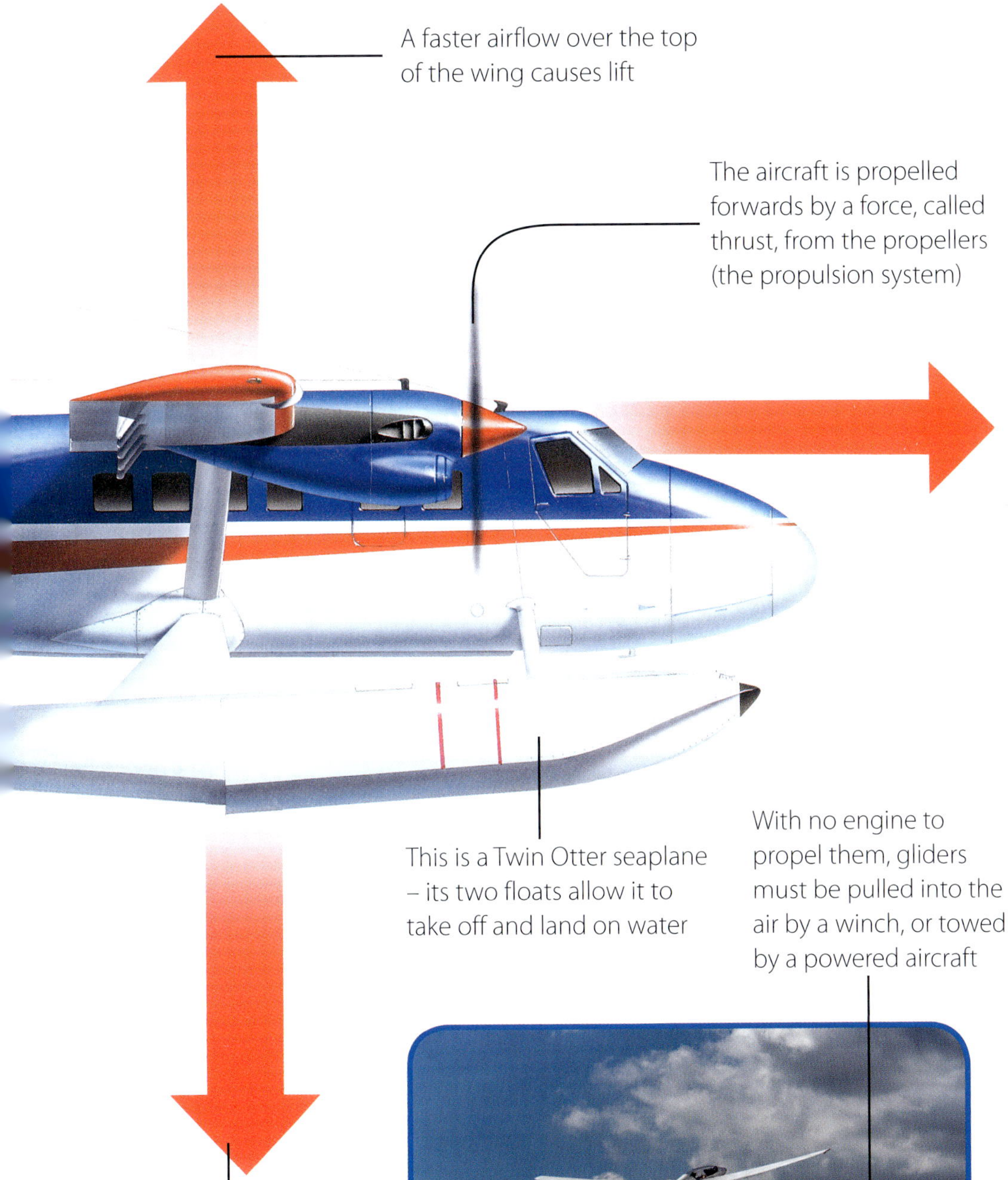

A faster airflow over the top of the wing causes lift

The aircraft is propelled forwards by a force, called thrust, from the propellers (the propulsion system)

This is a Twin Otter seaplane – its two floats allow it to take off and land on water

With no engine to propel them, gliders must be pulled into the air by a winch, or towed by a powered aircraft

Without lift, the weight of the aircraft would pull it down

Wings

As aircraft technology has developed, the shape of the wing in cross-section, called the aerofoil, has changed.

Early aviation pioneers used wings that were just flat sheets, set at an angle.

The Wright brothers made their wings cambered (curved) to generate more lift.

In World War II, heavy bombers had thick metal wings, which generated a lot of lift at low speeds

Early jet airliners had thinner wings, with slats and powerful flaps.

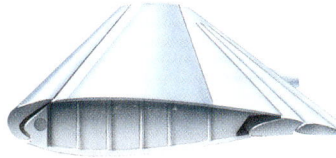

Some aircraft have 'super-critical' wings that are flatter on top and more curved underneath, which improves performance at both very high and low speeds.

The Controls

Inside the Boeing 747, or Jumbo Jet, there are more than 5,000 sets of control mechanisms. Pilots control the aeroplane with the help of a system of hinged parts called control surfaces. These control surfaces are moved by powerful hydraulic jacks. From the cockpit, the pilot sends commands through a mechanical system of cables to make the hydraulic jacks push, pull and rotate the surfaces.

The control surfaces include: ailerons (for roll); elevators (for climb and dive); rudder (for direction); spoilers (for roll and to act as airbrakes); and leading edge slats and trailing edge flaps (to give extra lift at low speeds, such as when the aeroplane is landing).

The cockpit

Most transport aircraft, like this Boeing 747, have a cockpit that seats two pilots (*see below right*). Each pilot has a set of controls. A control column is turned to roll the aircraft, or pushed or pulled to make it dive or climb, and there are pedals to operate the rudder.

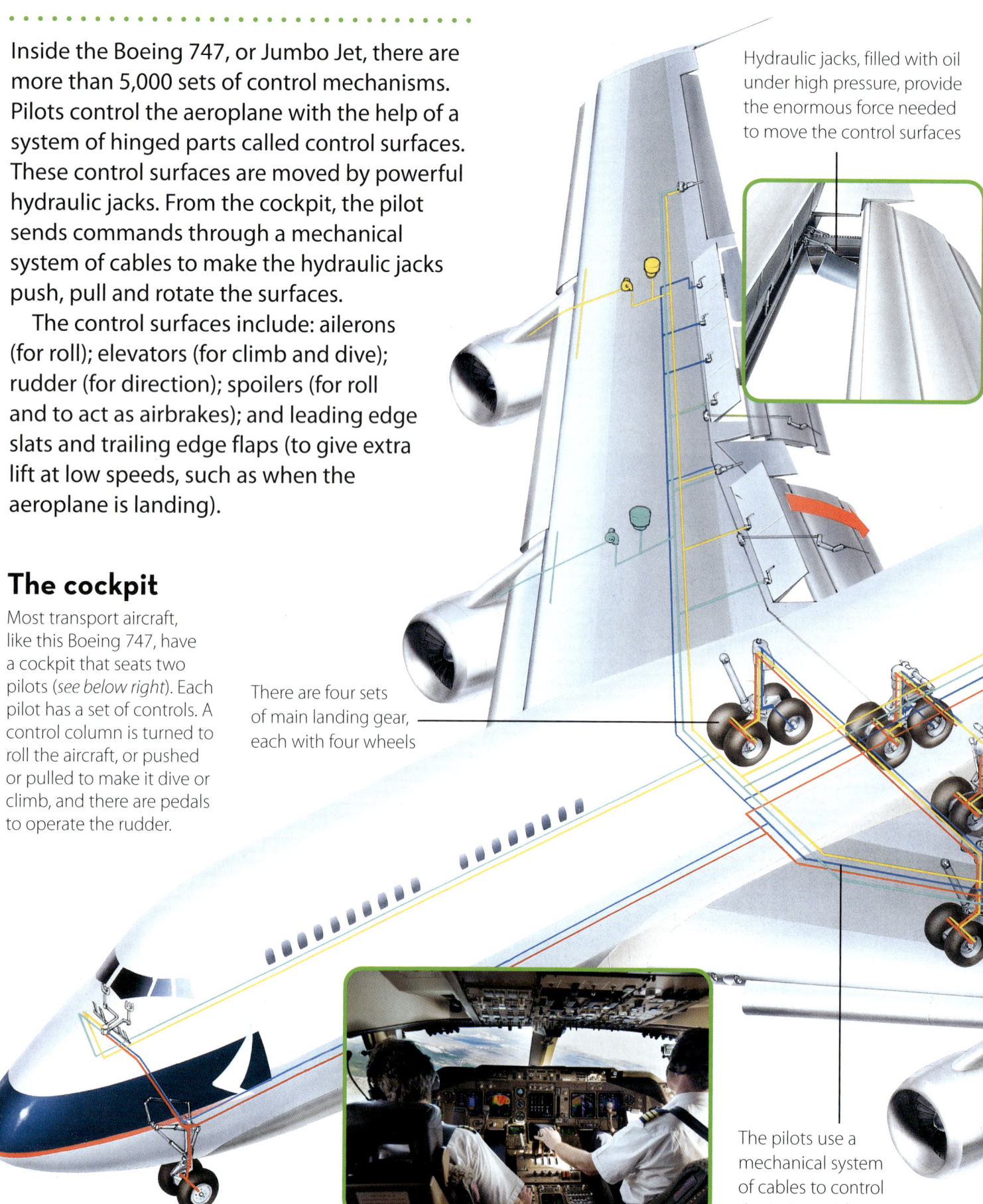

Hydraulic jacks, filled with oil under high pressure, provide the enormous force needed to move the control surfaces

There are four sets of main landing gear, each with four wheels

The pilots use a mechanical system of cables to control the jacks and flaps

Flying controls

Rolling (**1**) is done with ailerons and spoilers. Yawing – turning the nose left or right – is done with the rudder (**2**). To dive (**3**), the elevators are moved down. The elevators are moved up to make the aircraft climb (**4**).

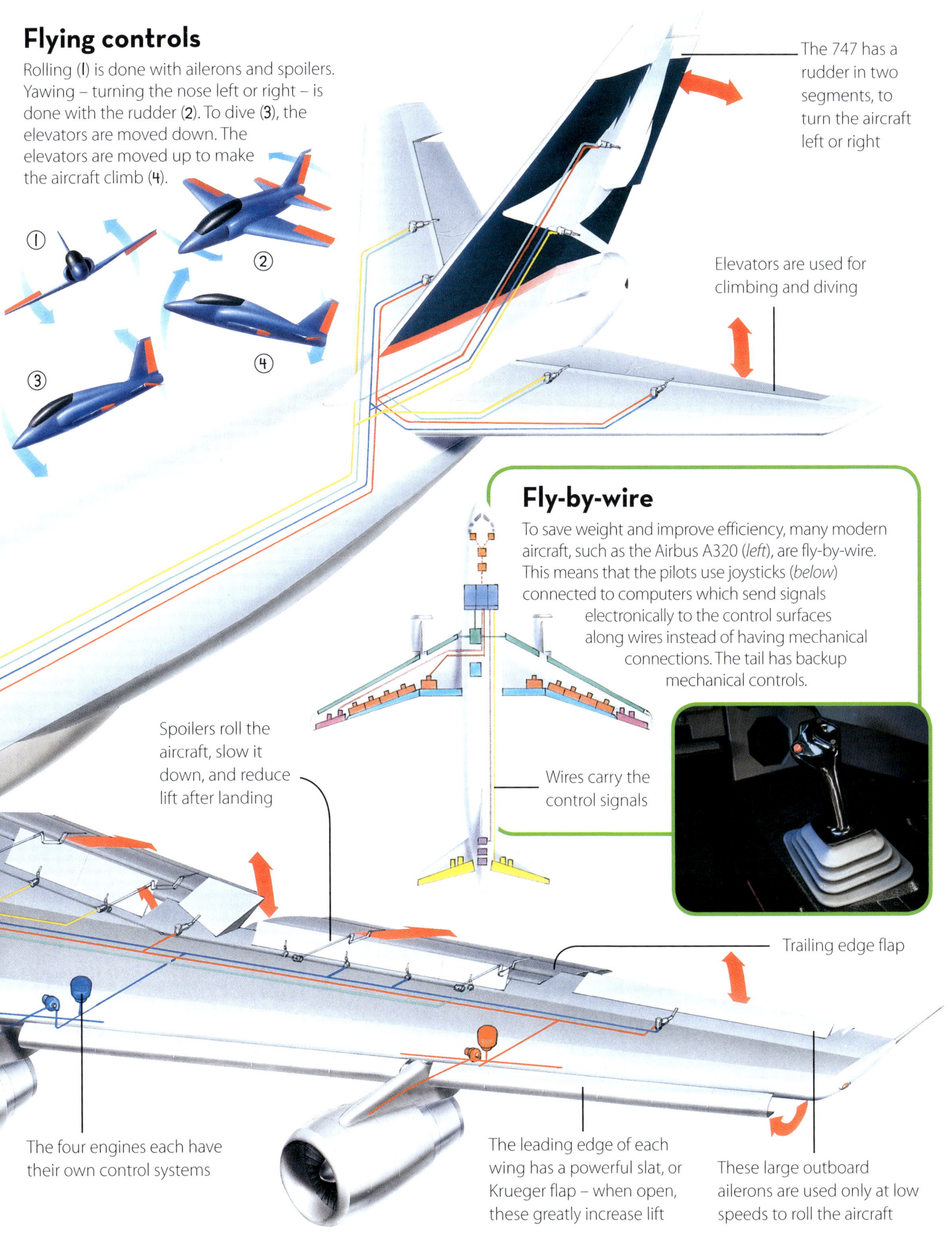

The 747 has a rudder in two segments, to turn the aircraft left or right

Elevators are used for climbing and diving

Fly-by-wire

To save weight and improve efficiency, many modern aircraft, such as the Airbus A320 (*left*), are fly-by-wire. This means that the pilots use joysticks (*below*) connected to computers which send signals electronically to the control surfaces along wires instead of having mechanical connections. The tail has backup mechanical controls.

Wires carry the control signals

Spoilers roll the aircraft, slow it down, and reduce lift after landing

Trailing edge flap

The four engines each have their own control systems

The leading edge of each wing has a powerful slat, or Krueger flap – when open, these greatly increase lift

These large outboard ailerons are used only at low speeds to roll the aircraft

Control Surfaces

The wing of a typical jet airliner changes shape before and after takeoff and before and after landing. To gain more lift on takeoff, the pilot extends huge flaps along the back (trailing edge) of the wing. Before landing, the pilot extends the flaps further, to increase lift even more as the aircraft slows down. On landing, spoilers are immediately raised to reduce lift and keep the aircraft down on the runway.

Small ailerons are raised or lowered to control the roll of the aircraft. Rolling or banking is necessary for turning. Further out along the wing are bigger ailerons, used only at low speeds. Along the front of the wing (leading edge) are slats, or flaps, which can also increase lift at low speeds.

The low-speed ailerons have 'static wicks' along the trailing edge to reduce static electricity

The outboard spoilers help to roll the aircraft and act as airbrakes

Fin and tailplane

An aeroplane's tail usually has a fin and a tailplane. A rudder is attached to the fin. hinged elevators are attached to the tailplane. In a multi-engined jet the rudder is not used much, except in cross-wind landings, or if an engine fails.

A 747's tail fin is over 20 metres high – three times as high as a house

Split rudders

Tailplane

This trailing edge flap is shown in the fully-down (landing) position

The small high-speed aileron is used throughout each flight

Elevators

Here, the trailing edge flap is seen from behind in the fully-down position

Flaps and spoilers

When a wing changes shape, the airflow is affected and the speed and direction of the aircraft is altered. Trailing edge flaps can be lowered to increase drag and slow the aircraft down (*below left*). The leading edge flaps are extended to give the extra lift needed at low speed. When spoilers are raised (*below right*), the airflow pushes the wing down, creating even more drag and reducing lift.

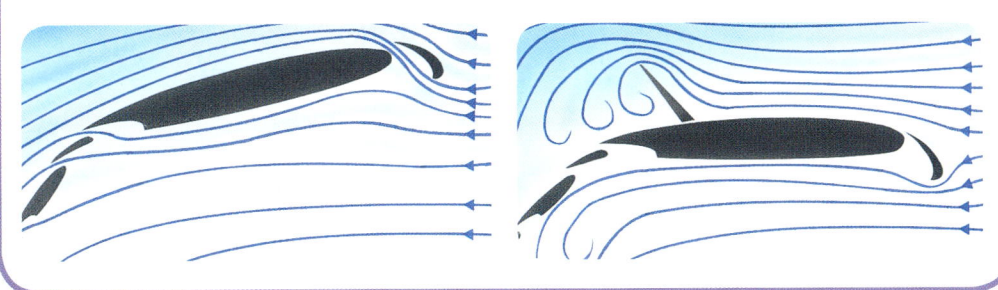

Hidden from view are ten sections of leading edge flap, which hinge down for takeoff or landing

The upper and lower wing skins are made from large sheets of metal

Inside the wing are ribs and spars which form huge fuel tanks

Rib

Spar

Two spoilers on each wing are raised to reduce wing lift and to slow the aircraft when landing

This is one of the hydraulic jacks that drive the spoilers

Inside the Cockpit

Early cockpits had very few instruments, but as aircraft developed and improved, it become more difficult for pilots of large aeroplanes to manage all of the aircraft's systems. Then came a revolutionary new cockpit (*right*).

The cockpit in the Airbus 340, which first flew in 1991, has six large screens on which the captain (sitting on the left) and the co-pilot (on the right) can see all the information they need. Overhead are the controls for the fuel, hydraulics, electrical systems, cabin pressurisation and air conditioning, as well as de-icing, emergency oxygen and other systems. The flight crew contols speed and direction with pedals and a sidestick held in one hand. Under the side windows are the nosewheel tillers for steering the Airbus on the ground. Below the windscreens are controls for the autopilot, which can keep the aeroplane on a set course.

The main warning display gives information about any possible failures

This panel controls the autopilot and other systems

Each pilot has a primary flight display – it shows the aircraft's speed, altitude and other information

Loudspeaker

Early cockpit

This is a cockpit from a 1930s biplane. There are just a few essential instruments. Two ignition switches are turned on before starting the engine. A compass for navigation is set into the bottom of the panel.

Ignition switches

Compass

Rudder pedals are used to apply the brakes after landing

The central console

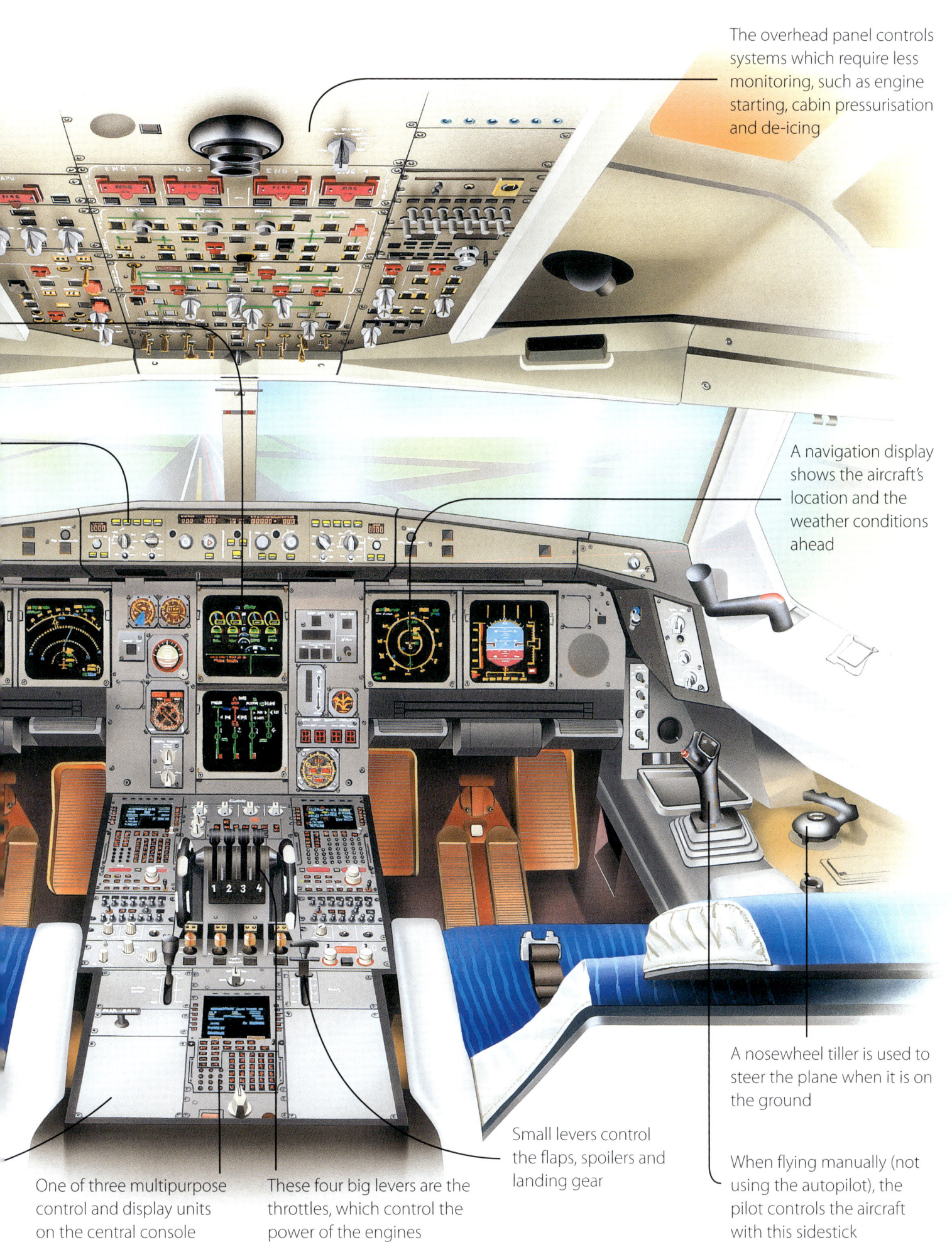

The overhead panel controls systems which require less monitoring, such as engine starting, cabin pressurisation and de-icing

A navigation display shows the aircraft's location and the weather conditions ahead

A nosewheel tiller is used to steer the plane when it is on the ground

When flying manually (not using the autopilot), the pilot controls the aircraft with this sidestick

Small levers control the flaps, spoilers and landing gear

One of three multipurpose control and display units on the central console

These four big levers are the throttles, which control the power of the engines

The Parts of an Aeroplane

Very few aeroplanes, such as the US Air Force B-2 Spirit stealth bomber, are just flying wings, without a body. Most have a body, called the fuselage, and a tail. The tail usually consists of a fixed vertical fin, to which the rudder is hinged, and a horizontal tailplane, on which the elevators are hinged.

One of the most successful jet fighters of recent times, the F-16 Fighting Falcon (*see right and bottom right*), has a pivoting tailplane. This is used instead of elevators for climbing and diving. The F-16's fuselage is packed with electronics, fuel tanks and the engine with its air duct. The pilot sits in a reclined (tilted backwards) ejection seat at the front. There is a perfect all-round view through the bubble canopy. The F-16 first flew in 1971 and around 3,000 are still in service. It is no longer made for the US Air Force, but F-16s are still built for other countries.

This is the starboard flaperon – it serves as both a flap and an aileron

The right (starboard) wing – each wing contains a fuel tank

In an emergency, the pilot's ejection seat can be used to propel the pilot safely away from the aircraft

The canopy

The cockpit

The enormous airflow needed by the engine is drawn in through this intake

An air data probe measures the speed of the F-16 through the air

Inside the fuselage is the large duct that carries air to the engine

The nose landing gear, which can be steered on the ground

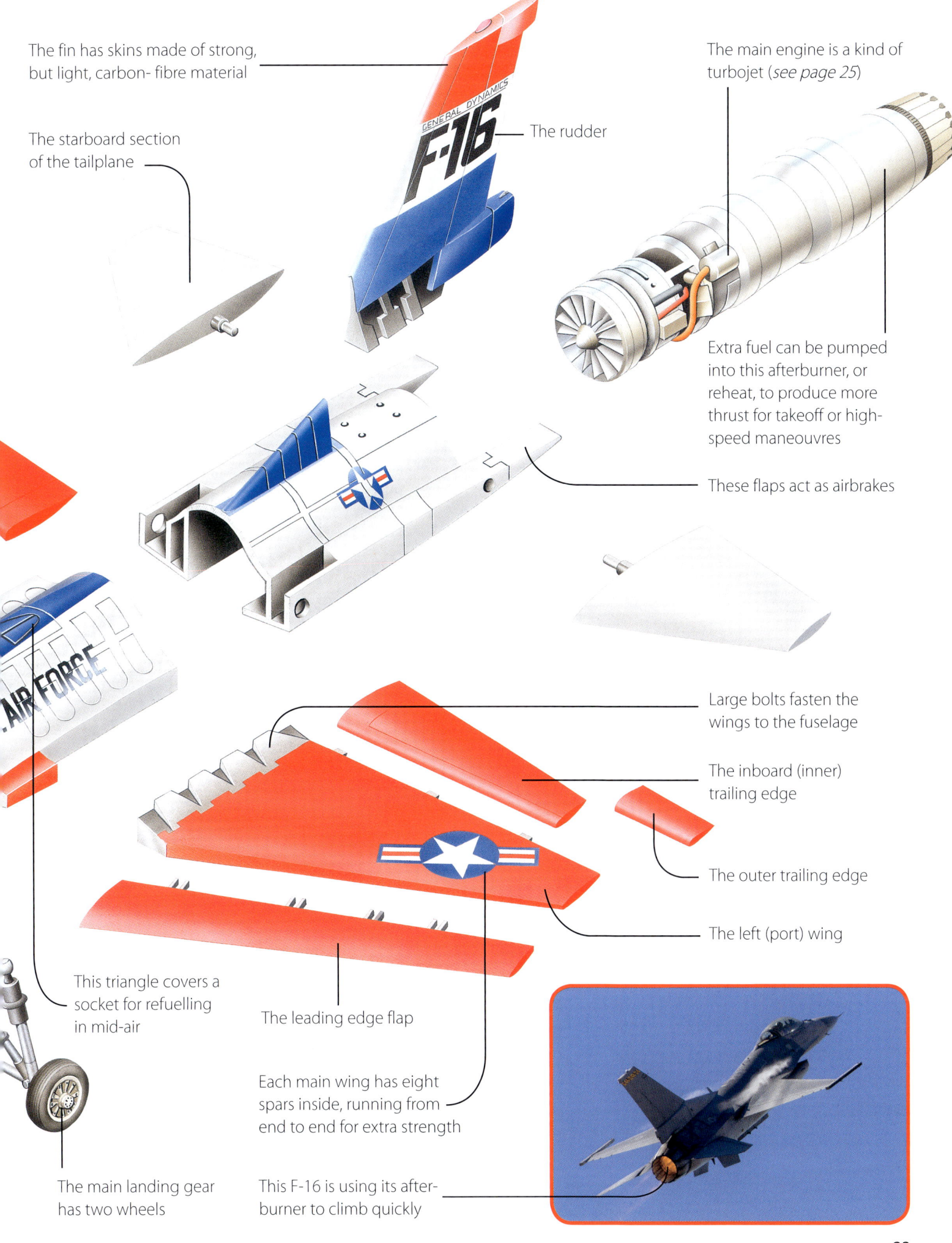

The fin has skins made of strong, but light, carbon- fibre material

The starboard section of the tailplane

The rudder

The main engine is a kind of turbojet (*see page 25*)

Extra fuel can be pumped into this afterburner, or reheat, to produce more thrust for takeoff or high-speed maneouvres

These flaps act as airbrakes

AIR FORCE

Large bolts fasten the wings to the fuselage

The inboard (inner) trailing edge

The outer trailing edge

The left (port) wing

This triangle covers a socket for refuelling in mid-air

The leading edge flap

Each main wing has eight spars inside, running from end to end for extra strength

The main landing gear has two wheels

This F-16 is using its afterburner to climb quickly

Engine Power

The first powered aircraft, such as the *Wright Flyer* (*see page 10*), used propellers which pushed them along. A propeller draws air from in front of it and throws it backwards. This drives the aircraft forwards. The jet of air thrown back by the propellers does not travel very fast, so the maximum recorded speed of a piston-engine propeller-powered aircraft is about 528 miles per hour (mph) or 840 km/h. Higher speeds can only be achieved by using different types of engines. Today, the fastest aircraft use turbojets or turbofans.

Piston engines

On smaller aircraft, such as the speed record-holding Grumman F8F-2 Bearcat 'Rare Bear' (*above*), propellers are usually driven by a piston engine, similar to a car's petrol engine. A Rolls-Royce Continental O-240A piston engine is shown below. Inside the engine are four cylinders, which each contain a piston. Fuel and air are burned to drive the pistons, which push the crankshaft round. The rotating crankshaft turns the propeller.

The thrust from the propeller pushes the aircraft along

The crankshaft rotates and turns the propeller

Rods join the pistons (which move to and fro) to the crankshaft (which rotates)

The camshaft turns cams which push rods to open the inlet and exhaust valves

The oil radiator is cooled by air flowing through it

The pistons inside the four cylinders are driven by a rapidly-burning petrol and air mixture

Each cylinder has an inlet valve, which lets in the petrol and air mixture, and an exhaust valve, through which exhaust gases escape

Turboprops

Some propellers are driven by a gas turbine engine, called a turboprop. Because these engines generate more power, some turboprop planes can reach speeds of more than 575 mph (925 km/h). The main shaft in a turboprop has to be slowed down, using gears like those in a car, because propellers waste power and make too much noise if they spin too fast. Many small airliners carrying 50–70 passengers are powered by two turboprops.

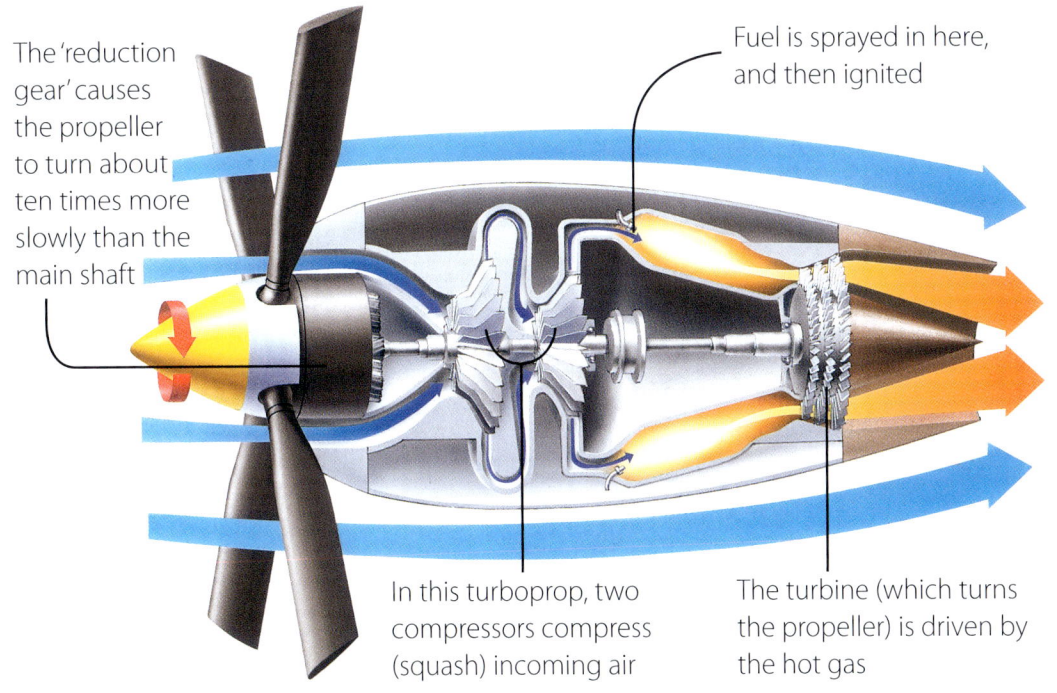

The 'reduction gear' causes the propeller to turn about ten times more slowly than the main shaft

Fuel is sprayed in here, and then ignited

The petrol and air mixture is fed into the engine through this pipe

In this turboprop, two compressors compress (squash) incoming air

The turbine (which turns the propeller) is driven by the hot gas

Turbojets

A more powerful gas turbine, the turbojet, was developed in 1937. Aircraft driven by turbojet engines do not have propellers. They are propelled by a backward jet of hot gas. These engines, usually in the form of turbofans (*see page 26*), propel the fastest larger aircraft.

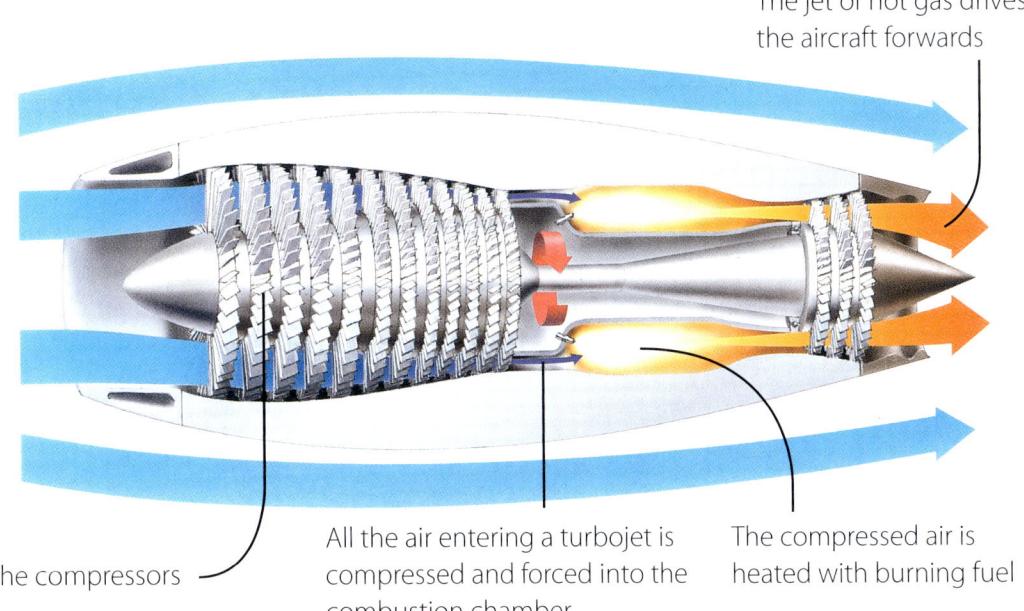

The jet of hot gas drives the aircraft forwards

This pipe discharges the exhaust gas from the engine

The compressors

All the air entering a turbojet is compressed and forced into the combustion chamber

The compressed air is heated with burning fuel

Jet Propulsion

A jet engine drives an aircraft forward with enormous force. Air is sucked in at the front, compressed by spinning blades and then mixed with fuel. This mixtures ignites, or burns, within the combustion chamber. The air is then expelled at high speed from the back. This stream of hot air – the 'jet' – causes thrust in the opposite direction (*see below*), propelling the aircraft forwards.

Most big airliners are powered by turbo-fan engines, which are quieter than other types of jet engine. Air is drawn in by a huge fan spinning at the front. Some of the air passes through the engine to thrust the aircraft forward, while most flows around the outside. The fan and compressor blades are themselves driven by turbines turned by the stream of hot air rushing out through the back of the engine.

Propulsion

Jet engines work on the principle of jet propulsion. An aircraft is propelled forwards because of a reaction to high-speed air travelling backwards. The same effect can be seen when you let go of the neck of a blown-up balloon. While the neck is pinched, the air pressure inside is the same in all directions, so the balloon remains still. Because the air is compressed inside, when you release the neck of the balloon the air will rush out at high speed. The air pressure at the opposite end to the neck is no longer counter-balanced, so the balloon flies forwards.

Engine mounting pylon

Spinning fan blades

Air is sucked in

A fan drives some of the air to flow around the outside of the engine, bypassing it

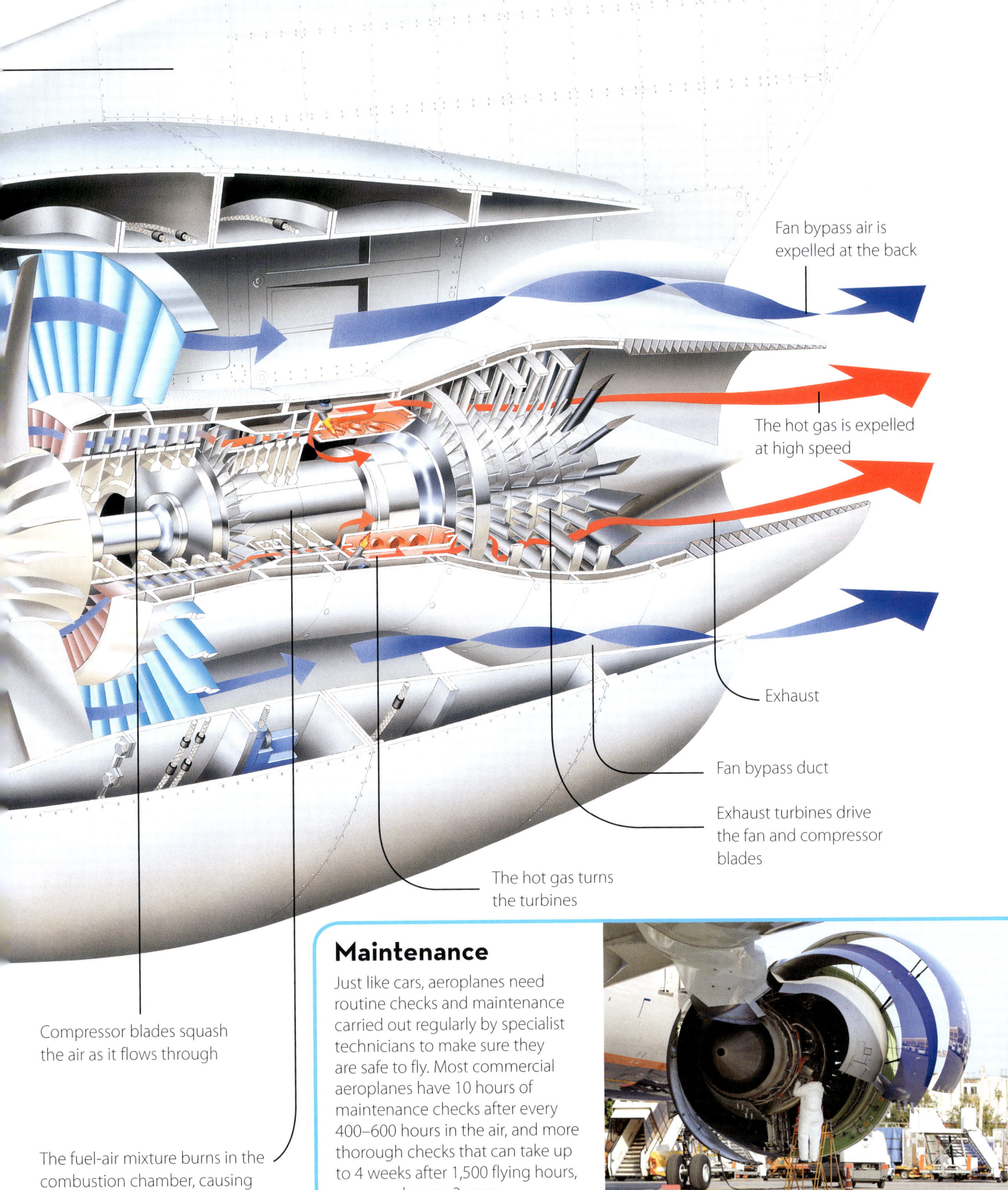

Fan bypass air is
expelled at the back

The hot gas is expelled
at high speed

Exhaust

Fan bypass duct

Exhaust turbines drive
the fan and compressor
blades

The hot gas turns
the turbines

Compressor blades squash
the air as it flows through

The fuel-air mixture burns in the
combustion chamber, causing
the gases to expand rapidly

Maintenance

Just like cars, aeroplanes need
routine checks and maintenance
carried out regularly by specialist
technicians to make sure they
are safe to fly. Most commercial
aeroplanes have 10 hours of
maintenance checks after every
400–600 hours in the air, and more
thorough checks that can take up
to 4 weeks after 1,500 flying hours,
or around every 2 years.

Power Systems

Like most large aircraft, the Boeing 747-400 is controlled by the flight crew via powerful electrical and hydraulic systems. The power needed to run these systems comes from fuel, carried in enormous tanks in the wings. The aircraft's four main engines burn fuel for flight, and also drive generators to make electricity. Two even more powerful electric generators are driven by the APU (*see above right*). Each engine also drives a hydraulic pump. Another four pumps are driven by high-pressure air. These pump hydraulic fluid to move the landing gear, flaps, flight controls, brakes and other systems. In the belly of the aircraft are the cabin pressurisation and air conditioning systems. When the aircraft is flying at high altitude, the air outside is too cold and too thin to breathe, so air for the passengers and crew in the cabin must be pressurised and kept warm.

APU

Most large passenger aircraft have an APU (auxiliary power unit). On the 747 it is at the tip of the tail end of the fuselage. It is a small gas turbine engine, like a miniature jet engine, which drives two electric generators. It also supplies compressed air to start the main engines and for air conditioning in the cabin. The arrows (*right*) show where air is sucked in and hot exhaust pushed out.

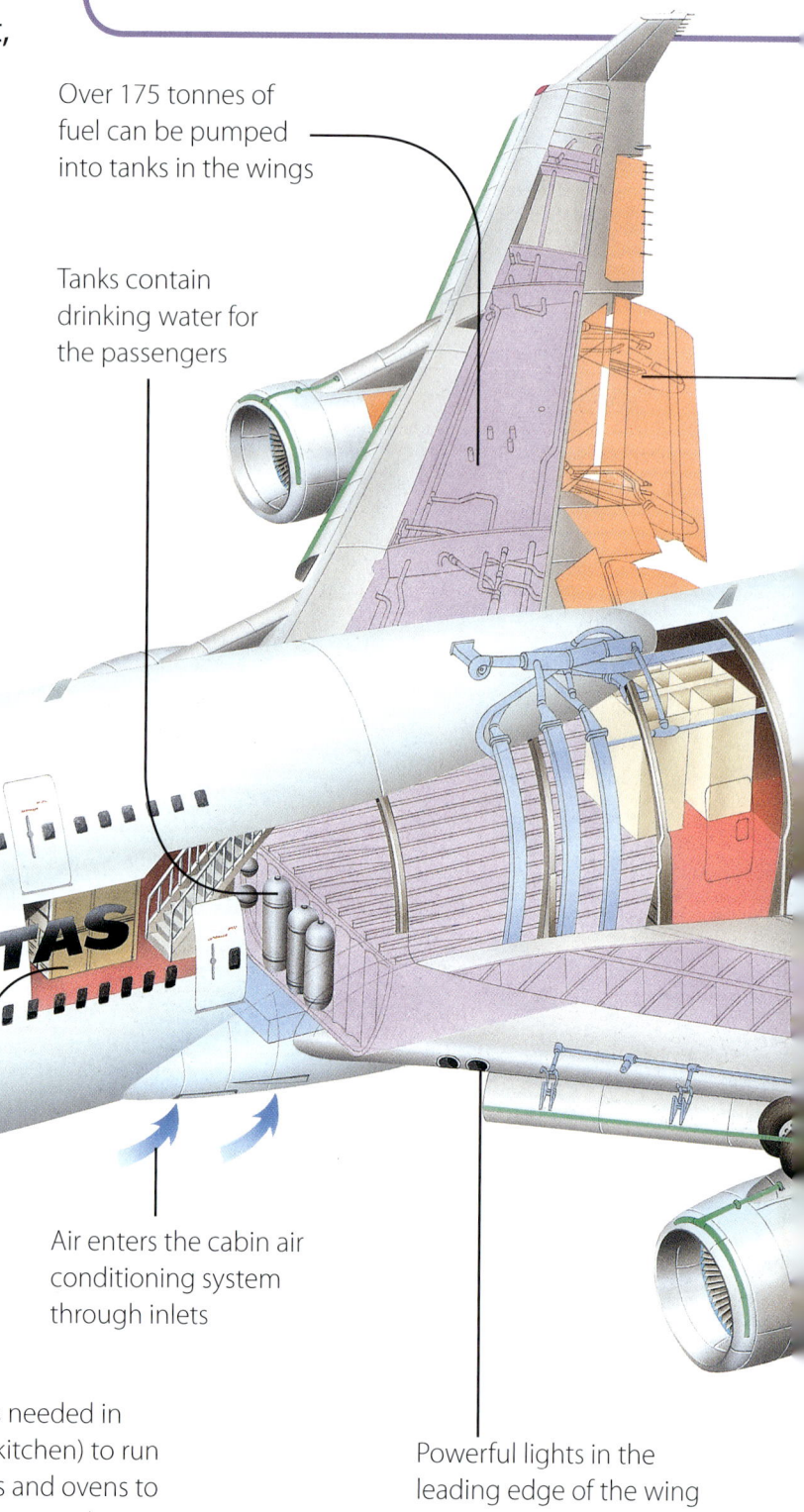

Over 175 tonnes of fuel can be pumped into tanks in the wings

Tanks contain drinking water for the passengers

Forward radar

Airtight pressure bulkhead

Air enters the cabin air conditioning system through inlets

Electricity is needed in the galley (kitchen) to run refrigerators and ovens to store and heat meals

Powerful lights in the leading edge of the wing are turned on for landing

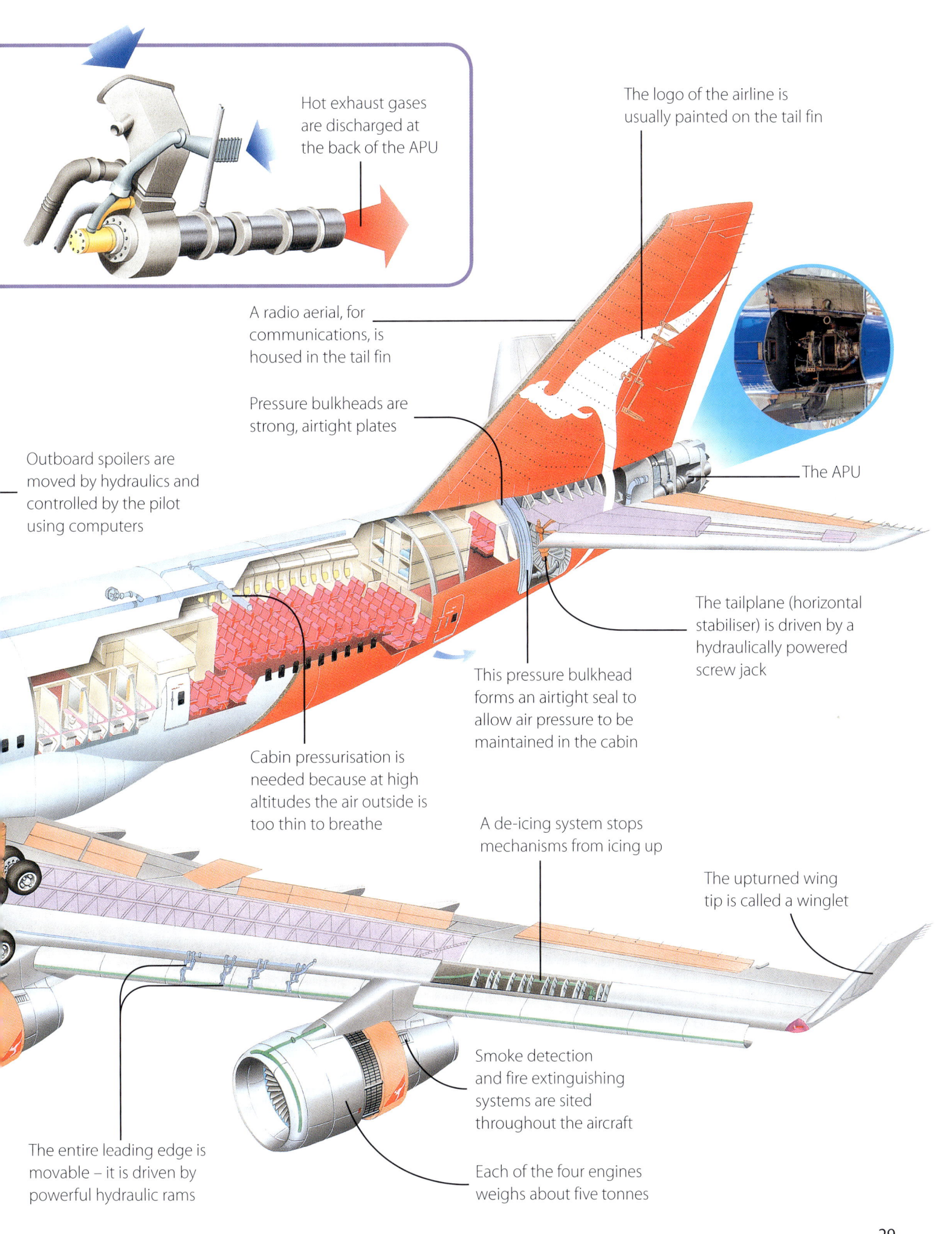

Hot exhaust gases are discharged at the back of the APU

The logo of the airline is usually painted on the tail fin

A radio aerial, for communications, is housed in the tail fin

Pressure bulkheads are strong, airtight plates

Outboard spoilers are moved by hydraulics and controlled by the pilot using computers

The APU

The tailplane (horizontal stabiliser) is driven by a hydraulically powered screw jack

This pressure bulkhead forms an airtight seal to allow air pressure to be maintained in the cabin

Cabin pressurisation is needed because at high altitudes the air outside is too thin to breathe

A de-icing system stops mechanisms from icing up

The upturned wing tip is called a winglet

Smoke detection and fire extinguishing systems are sited throughout the aircraft

The entire leading edge is movable – it is driven by powerful hydraulic rams

Each of the four engines weighs about five tonnes

29

Air Traffic Control

Like cars on a road, aircraft have to follow rules in order to avoid collisions. Large aircraft keep to invisible 'roads' in the sky, called Airways (at lower altitudes) or Upper Air Routes (at higher altitudes). Air traffic controllers at an airport work in a control tower (*see right*) where they monitor the progress of nearby aircraft on screens and by sight. Once they are on their way, other controllers guide aircraft from remote control centres. They can see which aircraft is which, at what altitude they are flying and the direction in which they are heading. Modern aircraft use GPS (Global Positioning System) navigation systems for guidance. When an aircraft reaches an airport, it may have to join a stack (like a queue) to await its turn to land.

ILS

An ILS (instrument landing system) sends signals to receiving equipment in aircraft to help them land safely, even in low cloud and fog. It consists of two radio beams sent from near the runway towards approaching air traffic. One guides the aircraft's direction (left or right). The other guides it vertically (up or down) along the correct glide path.

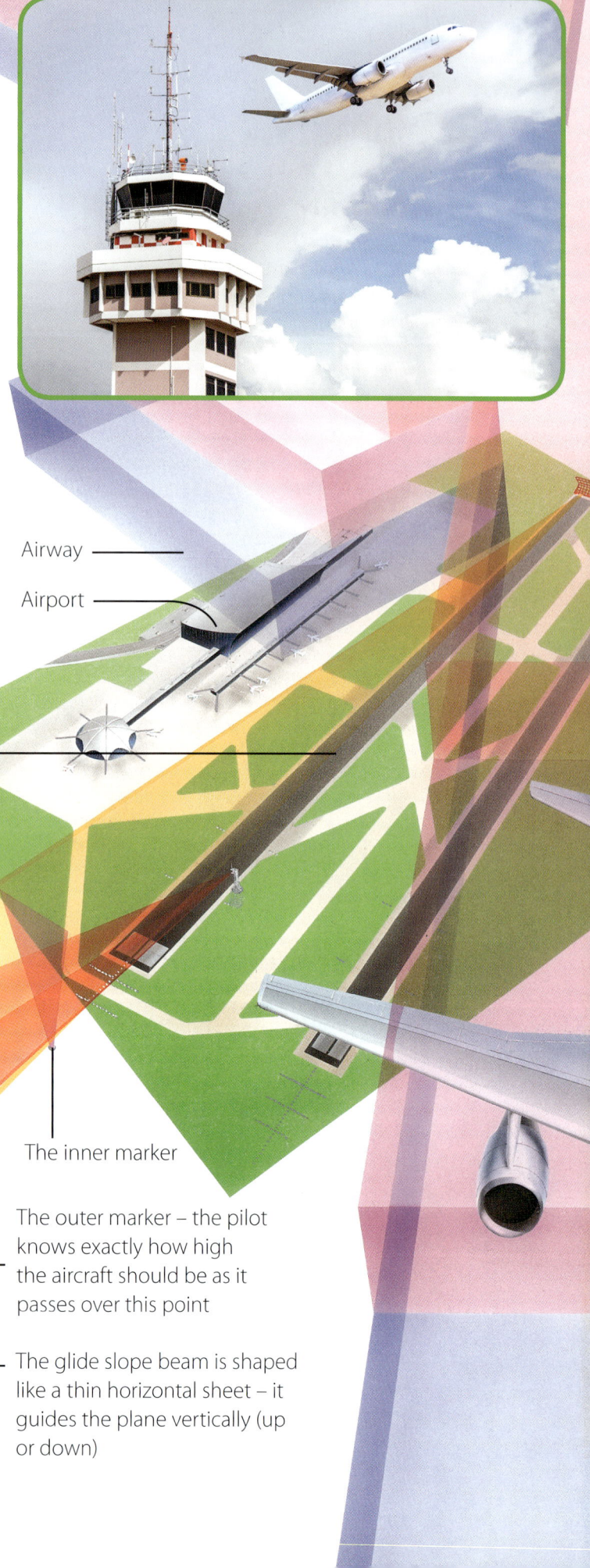

Airway

Airport

Runway

The centreline of an ILS runway – each approaching aircraft is guided to it in turn

The inner marker

The outer marker – the pilot knows exactly how high the aircraft should be as it passes over this point

The glide slope beam is shaped like a thin horizontal sheet – it guides the plane vertically (up or down)

An aircraft has 'captured' the two ILS beams and is being guided downwards

The localiser beam is shaped like a thin, vertical sheet and provides steering guidance (left or right)

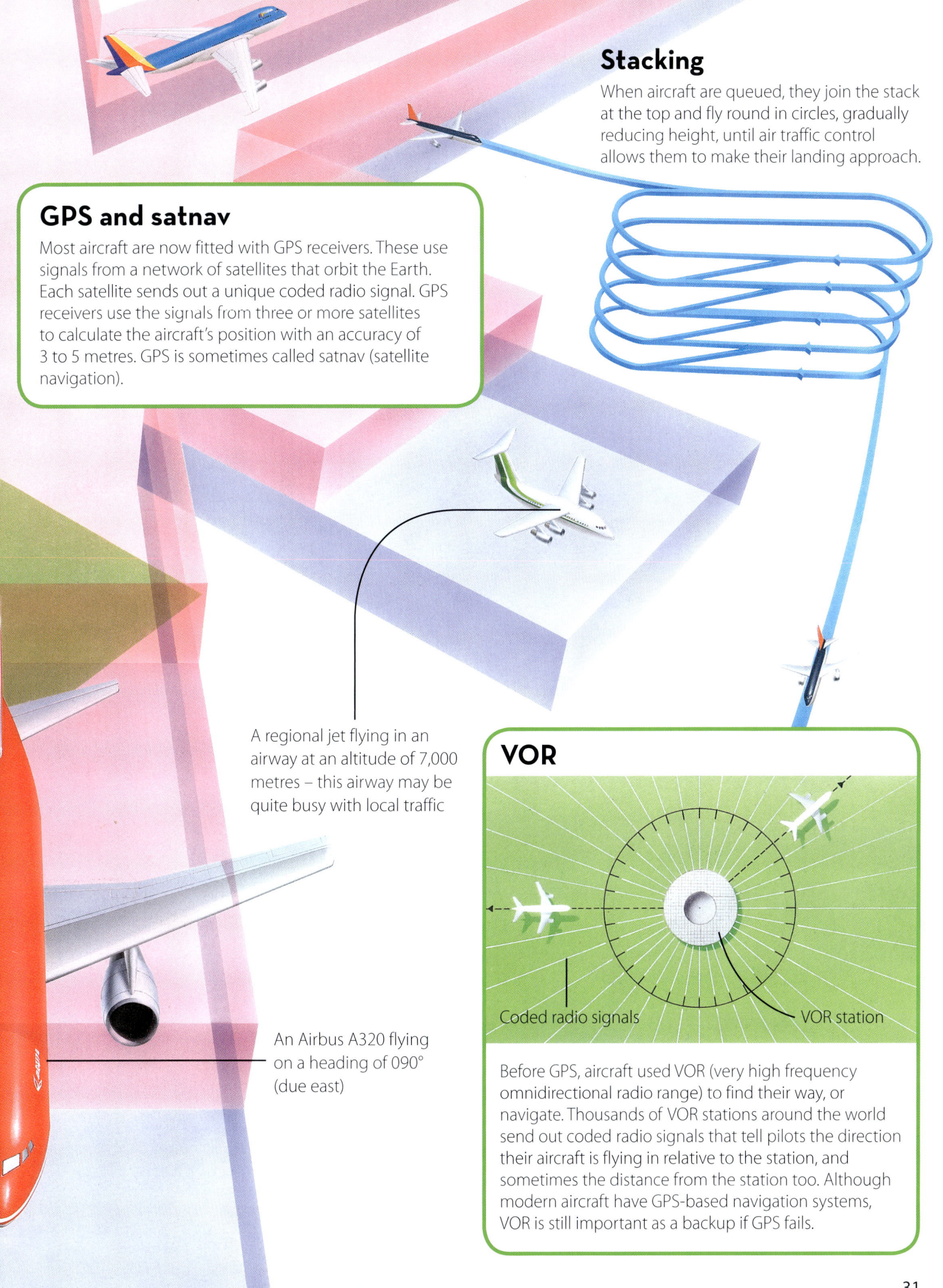

Stacking

When aircraft are queued, they join the stack at the top and fly round in circles, gradually reducing height, until air traffic control allows them to make their landing approach.

GPS and satnav

Most aircraft are now fitted with GPS receivers. These use signals from a network of satellites that orbit the Earth. Each satellite sends out a unique coded radio signal. GPS receivers use the signals from three or more satellites to calculate the aircraft's position with an accuracy of 3 to 5 metres. GPS is sometimes called satnav (satellite navigation).

A regional jet flying in an airway at an altitude of 7,000 metres – this airway may be quite busy with local traffic

An Airbus A320 flying on a heading of 090° (due east)

VOR

Coded radio signals

VOR station

Before GPS, aircraft used VOR (very high frequency omnidirectional radio range) to find their way, or navigate. Thousands of VOR stations around the world send out coded radio signals that tell pilots the direction their aircraft is flying in relative to the station, and sometimes the distance from the station too. Although modern aircraft have GPS-based navigation systems, VOR is still important as a backup if GPS fails.

Radar

Radar uses radio beams to detect objects at a great distance, even at night or through clouds. Huge radar stations on the ground monitor the progress of every aircraft in the sky for hundreds of kilometres in all directions. Most big or powerful aircraft carry their own radar. The main radar will be in the nose, looking ahead, like a car headlamp. A passenger jet's radar scans the flight path for mountains, for other aircraft at the same height (to avoid them) and especially for thunderstorms and clouds, which could throw the aircraft around and make passengers feel airsick. By checking the radar screens, the pilot is able to 'see' far ahead, so they can steer around turbulence (changes in the movement of air outside the aircraft that can make the flight feel bumpy).

Military aircraft often have a backward-facing radar as well, to warn if an enemy plane is trying to approach them from behind. There are also specialised types of radar that can produce detailed pictures of the ground below an aircraft.

Radar beams are sent out and received back by this dish-shaped antenna

The radar is housed inside the aircraft's nose cone

Radar location

The most common place for an aircraft's radar is in its nose. From here it is able to scan the horizon to detect obstacles or bad weather ahead of the aircraft.

The jet's radar beam checks the sky ahead

The jet can be seen by air traffic control radar on the ground

Radar altimeter

Smaller aircraft use altimeters that measure air pressure, which decreases with height. However, pressure altimeters only measure an aircraft's altitude compared to sea level, not to the height of the ground below them. They cannot tell if an aircraft flying at 300 metres altitude is heading towards a 600 metre-high mountain. A radar altimeter measures the exact distance to the ground and would detect the rising land level on approach to a mountain. Radar altimeters are also used by passenger aircraft and military planes when landing.

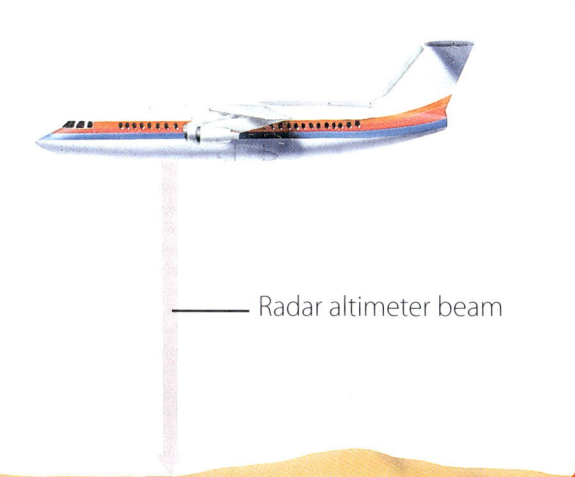

Radar altimeter beam

Without radar, the pilot would not be able to tell if there was violent turbulence inside a cloud, even in daylight

Radar images

The first image (1) shows how radar warns the pilot of severe turbulence inside clouds (here it is shown in red). The other radar screen (2) shows ground features, such as hills and coastlines.

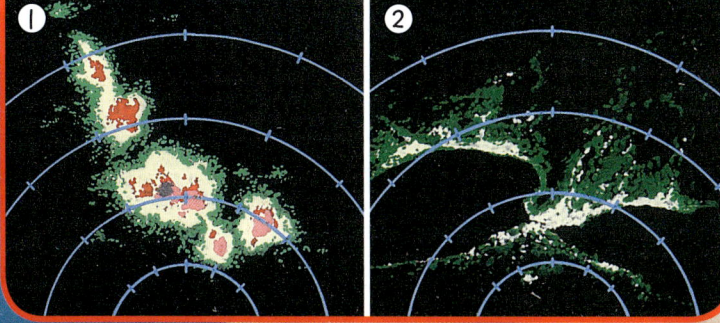

Supersonic Aircraft

Sound travels through the air at a speed of about 767 mph (1,235 km/h). In 1947, an American, Chuck Yeager, piloted the first aeroplane to fly faster than sound (or Mach 1). Aircraft able to do this are called supersonic, or hypersonic if they fly faster than five times the speed of sound (Mach 5). In 1959, an X-15 aeroplane (*below*) made its first flight. Powered by a rocket, the X-15 was capable of reaching speeds of up to 4,520 mph (7,274 km/h), or Mach 6.7. This speed was achieved in October 1967 and is still the fastest recorded manned flight, although in 2004 NASA's unmanned NASA X-43A aircraft (*bottom right*) reached a speed of Mach 9.6, almost 10 times the speed of sound. In 1969, Concorde, the world's first supersonic passenger aircraft, took its first flight. It was in service between 1976 and 2003 and 20 Concordes were built.

Subsonic flight

These circles represent the sound waves made by the aircraft's engines

The diagram above shows how the Concorde supersonic airliner flew at subsonic speed (slower than sound). The sound waves spread away like ripples on a pond, those in front of the nose travelling away from it. This happens with all subsonic aircraft. The noise of their engines rushes away from them much faster than they can fly.

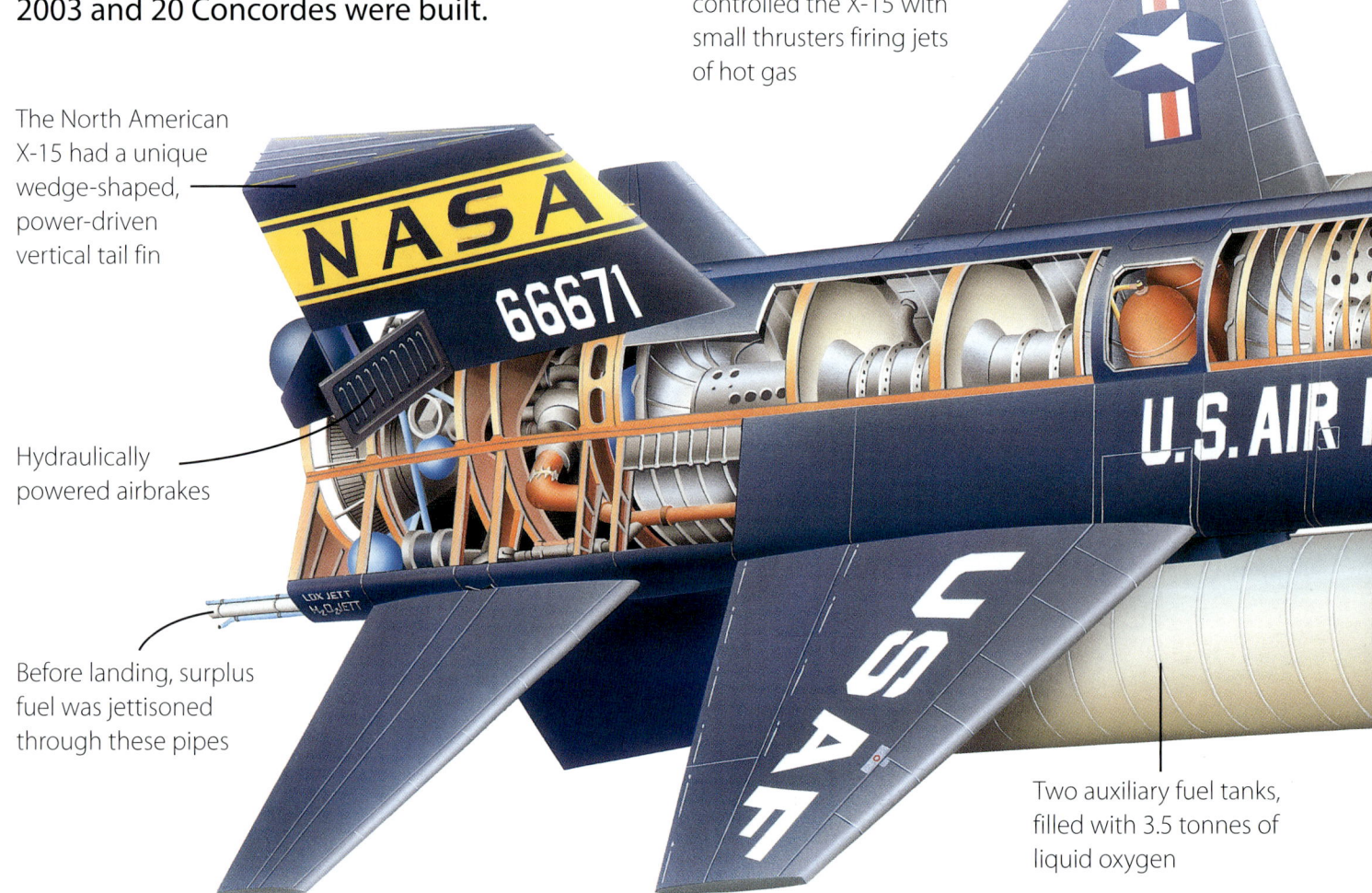

In airless space the pilot controlled the X-15 with small thrusters firing jets of hot gas

The North American X-15 had a unique wedge-shaped, power-driven vertical tail fin

Hydraulically powered airbrakes

Before landing, surplus fuel was jettisoned through these pipes

Two auxiliary fuel tanks, filled with 3.5 tonnes of liquid oxygen

At the speed of sound

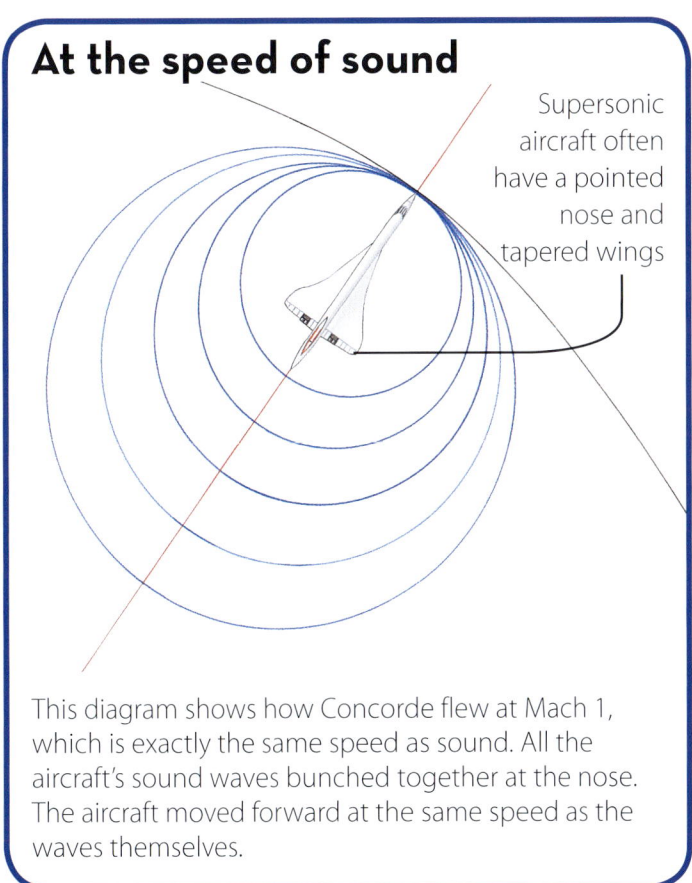

Supersonic aircraft often have a pointed nose and tapered wings

This diagram shows how Concorde flew at Mach 1, which is exactly the same speed as sound. All the aircraft's sound waves bunched together at the nose. The aircraft moved forward at the same speed as the waves themselves.

Mach 2

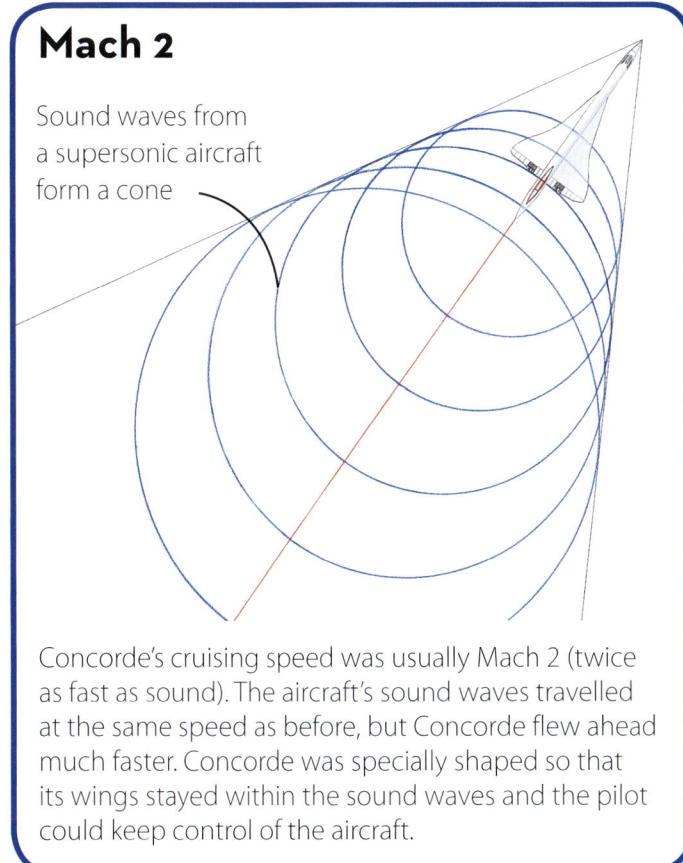

Sound waves from a supersonic aircraft form a cone

Concorde's cruising speed was usually Mach 2 (twice as fast as sound). The aircraft's sound waves travelled at the same speed as before, but Concorde flew ahead much faster. Concorde was specially shaped so that its wings stayed within the sound waves and the pilot could keep control of the aircraft.

Ammonia kept in this tank was mixed with the liquid oxygen to drive the rocket engine

The X-15 was made of a nickel alloy that retained its strength even at extreme temperatures

The tip of the nose became white-hot in flight

PU EXHAUST

MAJ W. KNIGHT

RESCUE

HYD DRAIN

X-15

RCE

The only wheels were twin nosewheels, which were tucked away during flight

Parachutes were used to drop the fuel tanks safely so they could be used again

The tiny X-43A aircraft was launched from a Boeing B-52 Stratofortress and taken up to 33,000 metres (110,000 feet) by its Pegasus carrier rocket, where it ignited its scramjet engine

VTOL Aircraft

When taking off from the ground, ordinary aircraft have to travel down a long runway to build up enough speed for their wings to generate sufficient lift to get airborne. They also need runways in order to land safely.

Until 1960, only helicopters could take off or land in a small space without a runway. In 1960, a British team of engineers produced a prototype aircraft with one jet engine with two nozzles on each side. The nozzles could be rotated to point downwards to give the aircraft lift, or backwards to propel it forward. This allowed it to perform vertical takeoff and landing, or VTOL, and led to the development of the Harrier (*right*). It first flew in 1967 and remains the only true VTOL warplane. Some Harriers are still in use on naval aircraft carriers today, but many have been replaced by the short takeoff and vertical landing (STOVL) version of the F-35 Lightning II (*below*).

Harrier and V-22 Osprey

The Harrier (*right, top*) has a special turbofan engine with four nozzles, two on each side. These can swivel and point down to lift the Harrier. When they point backwards, they can drive it forward at almost the speed of sound. The V-22 Osprey (*right, bottom*) can also land and take off vertically. It has two big prop-rotors. When they are tilted up, they act like the rotors of a helicopter and lift the Osprey. When tilted forwards, they act like propellers and allow it to fly at up to 351 mph (565 km/h). The Osprey can do everything a helicopter can, but it can fly twice as fast and more than twice as far.

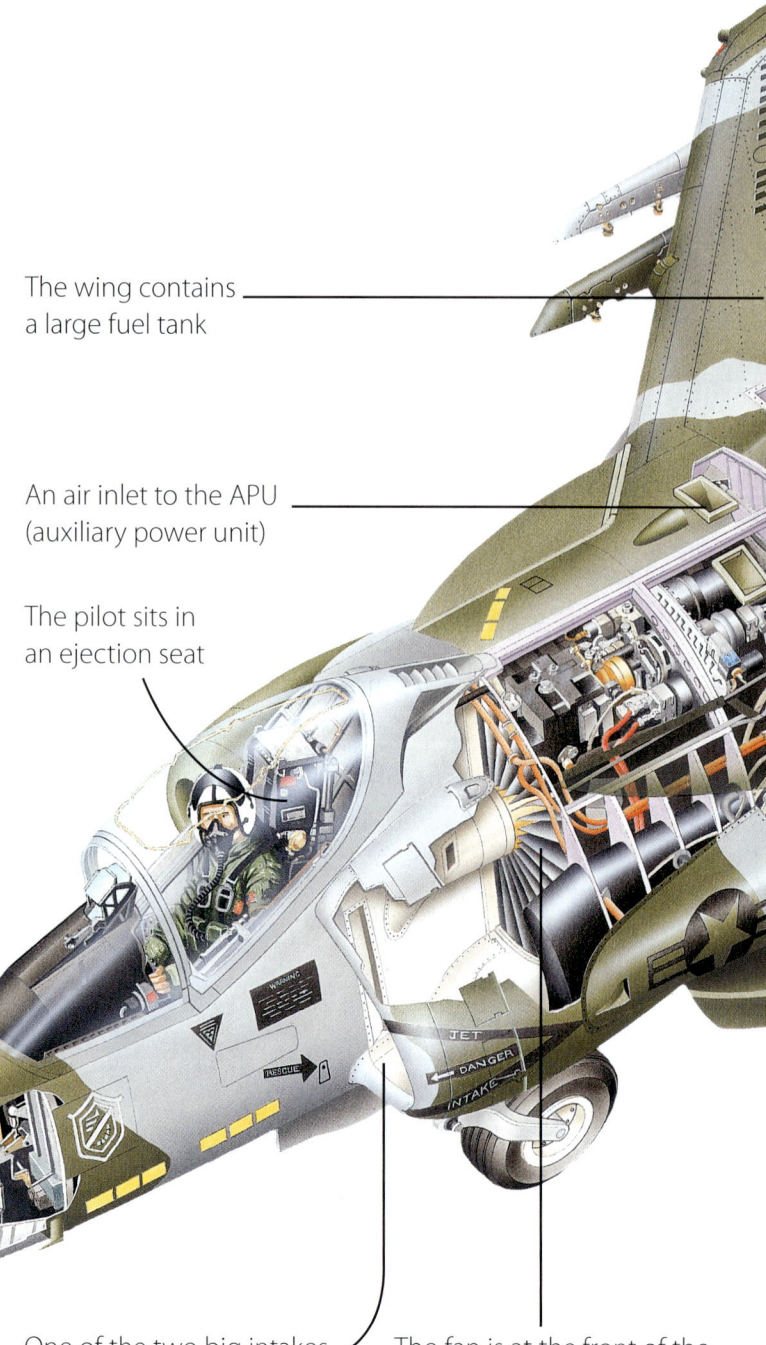

The wing contains a large fuel tank

An air inlet to the APU (auxiliary power unit)

The pilot sits in an ejection seat

The F-35 Lightning II's engine nozzle rotates to point downwards to make a vertical landing on an aircraft carrier

The nose of the Harrier is filled with avionics (aviation electronics)

One of the two big intakes that feed air to the engine

The fan is at the front of the Rolls-Royce Pegasus engine

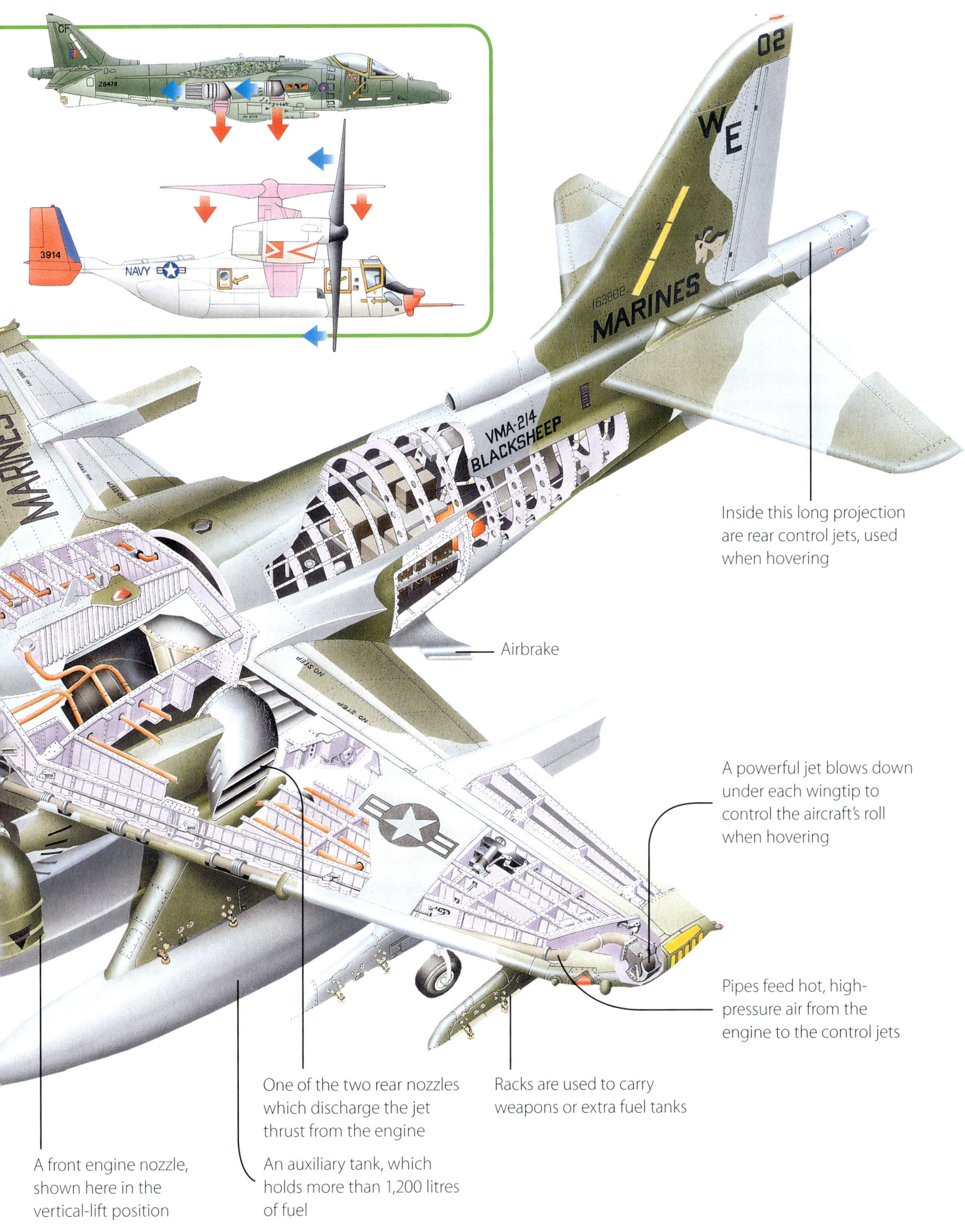

Inside this long projection are rear control jets, used when hovering

Airbrake

A powerful jet blows down under each wingtip to control the aircraft's roll when hovering

Pipes feed hot, high-pressure air from the engine to the control jets

One of the two rear nozzles which discharge the jet thrust from the engine

Racks are used to carry weapons or extra fuel tanks

A front engine nozzle, shown here in the vertical-lift position

An auxiliary tank, which holds more than 1,200 litres of fuel

Microlights

Since the early days of flight, many designers have tried to create small, affordable light aircraft. Around 1960, a new kind of wing, called the Rogallo, was introduced which made the now popular sport of hang gliding possible. It was shaped like a triangle, flying point-first. A light framework of metal tubing was added underneath to support a person's weight. These gliders led in turn to the development of small powered aeroplanes, or 'microlights'. The pilot sits on or inside a tiny craft with a pusher engine at the back. Some of these microlights still have Rogallo wings, but today most have simple rigid wings. The modern 'micro' consists of a wing and a 'trike unit' (so called because it has three wheels).

Autogyros, which have a rotor instead of a wing, have also been developed. These are powered by a small engine which drives a propeller at the back of the autogyro. The aircraft's forward motion causes air to rush past the rotor blades, spinning them round, which creates lift.

Autogyros

The autogyro was invented by Spanish engineer Juan de la Cierva in an attempt to create an aircraft that could fly safely at low speeds. He first flew one on 9 January 1923, at Cuatro Vientos Airfield in Madrid. The pilot sat in a streamlined pod with an open cockpit and had to wear a helmet and goggles for safety. Modern autogyros have enclosed cockpits, and some can be driven on roads, or have floats to land on water.

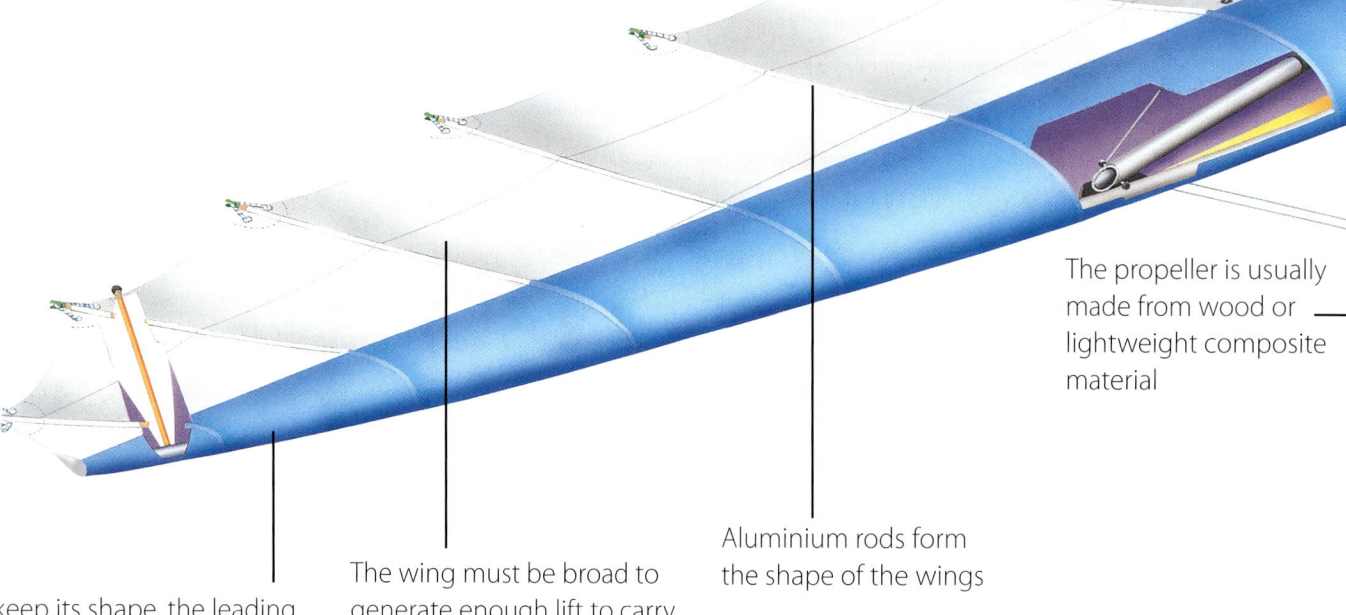

The propeller is usually made from wood or lightweight composite material

Aluminium rods form the shape of the wings

The wing must be broad to generate enough lift to carry the pilot and trike unit

To keep its shape, the leading edge is usually stiffened with kevlar or plastic

The rudder is used to steer the microlight in the right direction

Cords attach each of the wing rods to the trailing edge

The wing and trike unit join at the A-frame

Strong wires or cables support the weight of the trike and pilot

The pilot mainly controls the microlight by manoeuvering the A-frame

Some models can carry a passenger as well as the pilot

The small piston engine develops up to 75 kW of power (approximately 100 horsepower)

Sprung shock absorbers on the main wheels help to give a soft landing

The trike unit is usually made of fibreglass

The wheels have brakes to stop on the ground

This nose gear can be steered on the ground

PEGASUS

Human-Powered Aircraft

The first human-powered aircraft was flown in 1961, over a distance of 650 metres. Designs and flight distances have since improved greatly, as lighter but stronger materials – such as titanium, carbon fibre, glass fibre, low-density plastic foam and thin transparent film – have become available. The wing must have an enormous span, – around 30 metres from tip to tip – but be very light. The pilot has to pedal to gain enough speed to take off, driving the large propeller through rotating shafts and gear wheels. A champion cyclist is needed if a human-powered aircraft is to be flown a long way. The *Daedalus 88,* shown here, holds the distance record for human-powered flight – 71.5 miles (115 kilometres).

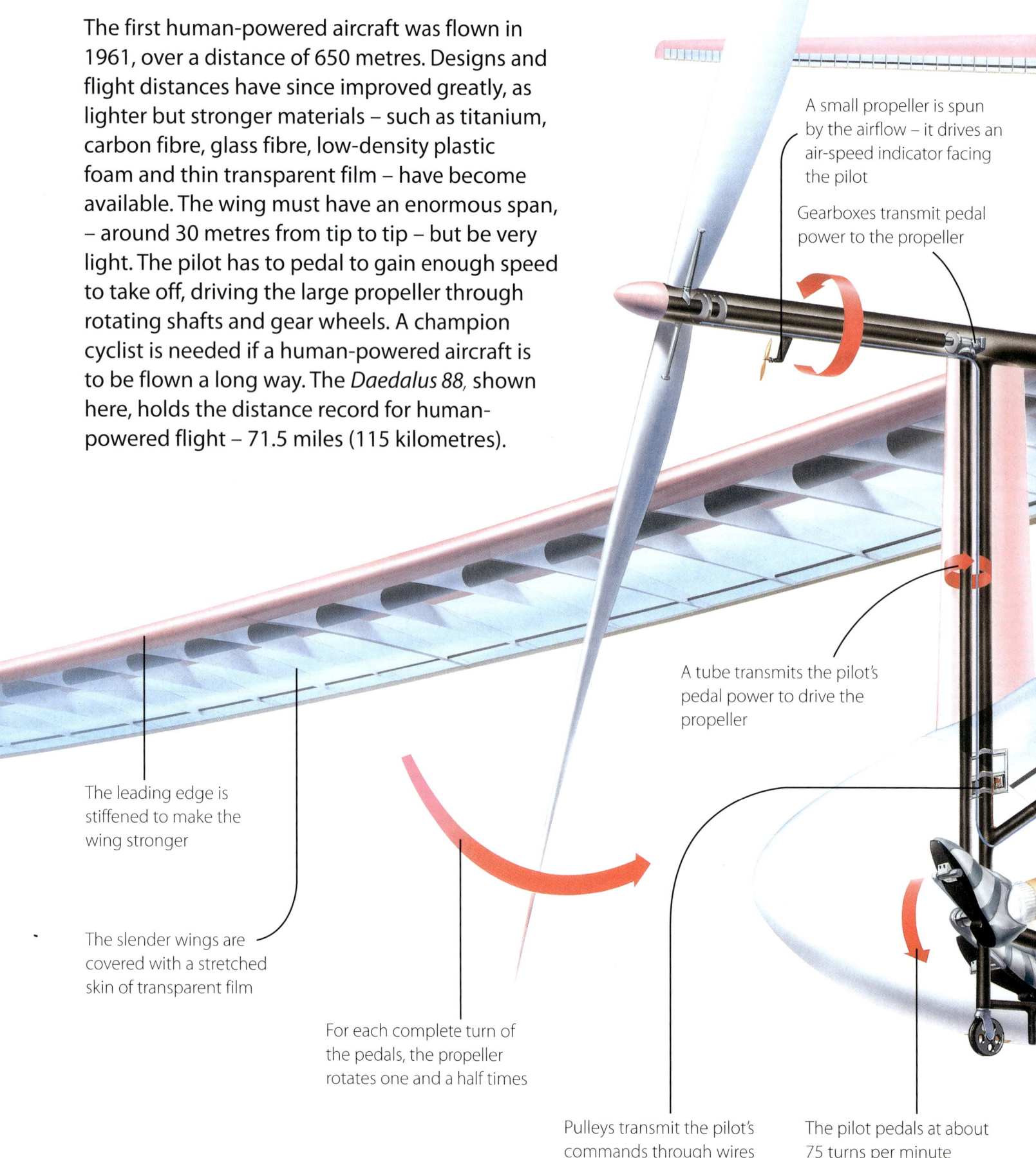

A small propeller is spun by the airflow – it drives an air-speed indicator facing the pilot

Gearboxes transmit pedal power to the propeller

A tube transmits the pilot's pedal power to drive the propeller

The leading edge is stiffened to make the wing stronger

The slender wings are covered with a stretched skin of transparent film

For each complete turn of the pedals, the propeller rotates one and a half times

Pulleys transmit the pilot's commands through wires

The pilot pedals at about 75 turns per minute

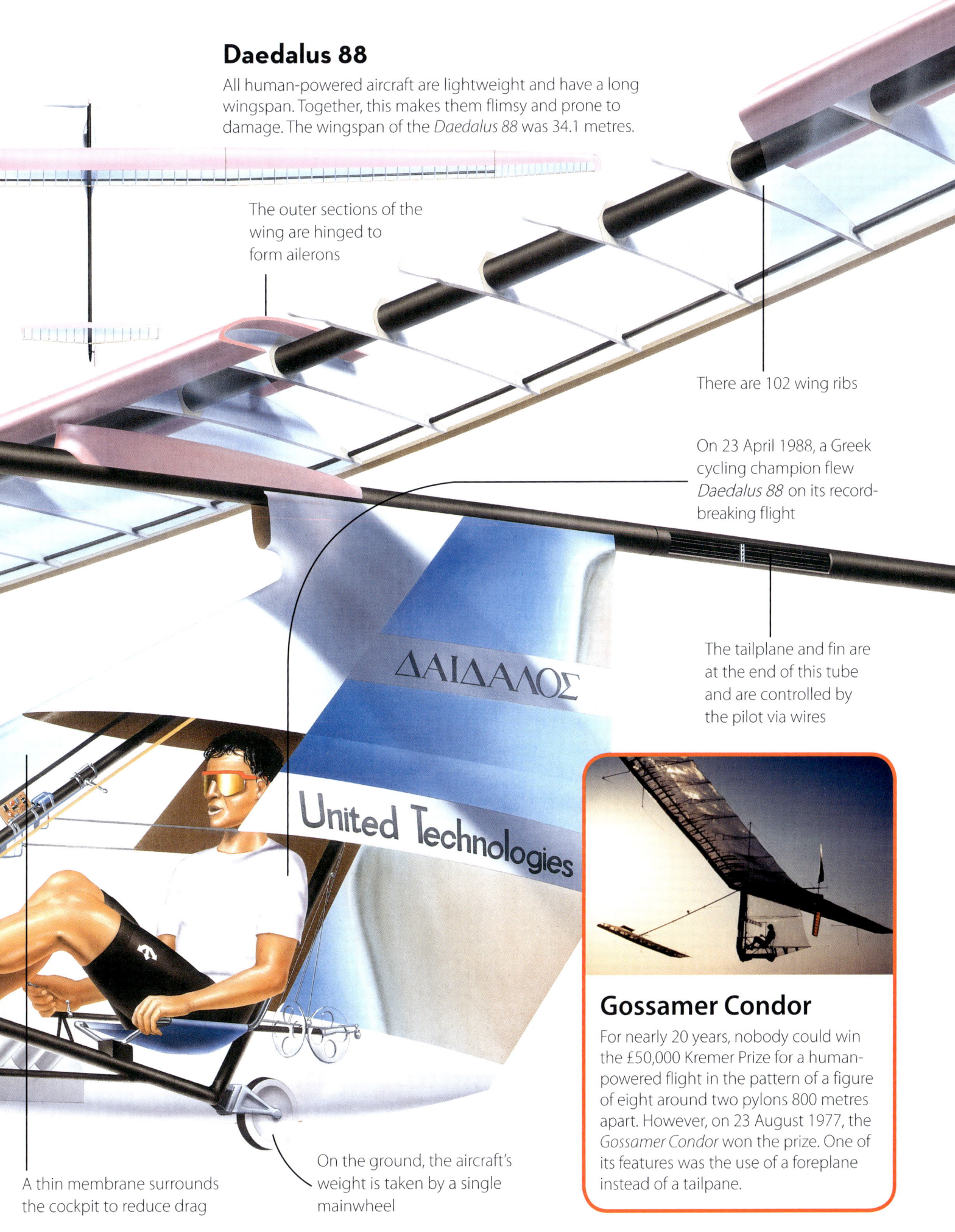

Daedalus 88

All human-powered aircraft are lightweight and have a long wingspan. Together, this makes them flimsy and prone to damage. The wingspan of the *Daedalus 88* was 34.1 metres.

The outer sections of the wing are hinged to form ailerons

There are 102 wing ribs

On 23 April 1988, a Greek cycling champion flew *Daedalus 88* on its record-breaking flight

ΔΑΙΔΑΛΟΣ

United Technologies

The tailplane and fin are at the end of this tube and are controlled by the pilot via wires

Gossamer Condor

For nearly 20 years, nobody could win the £50,000 Kremer Prize for a human-powered flight in the pattern of a figure of eight around two pylons 800 metres apart. However, on 23 August 1977, the *Gossamer Condor* won the prize. One of its features was the use of a foreplane instead of a tailpane.

A thin membrane surrounds the cockpit to reduce drag

On the ground, the aircraft's weight is taken by a single mainwheel

Helicopter Flight

Helicopters do not appear to have wings, but in fact their wings are long and thin, and spin round and round, forming what is called a rotor. Helicopters are also called rotary-winged aircraft. This helicopter (*below*) is a Sikorsky Seahawk of the United States Navy, which first flew in 1974 and is still in active service. It has a four-blade main rotor. Its four rotating wings lift it off the ground and propel it forwards or backwards. An upright rotor on the tail at the back pushes the tail sideways. This stops the main rotor from spinning the fuselage round in circles, adding stability and manoeuvrability. The rotors are driven by two powerful engines, one mounted on each side of the helicopter's fuselage.

Each turboshaft engine develops more than 1,600 horsepower and weighs 220 kg

Controls linking the cockpit to the rotors

Rear-view mirror

The pilot sits on the right, next to the tactical controller, who can also fly the helicopter

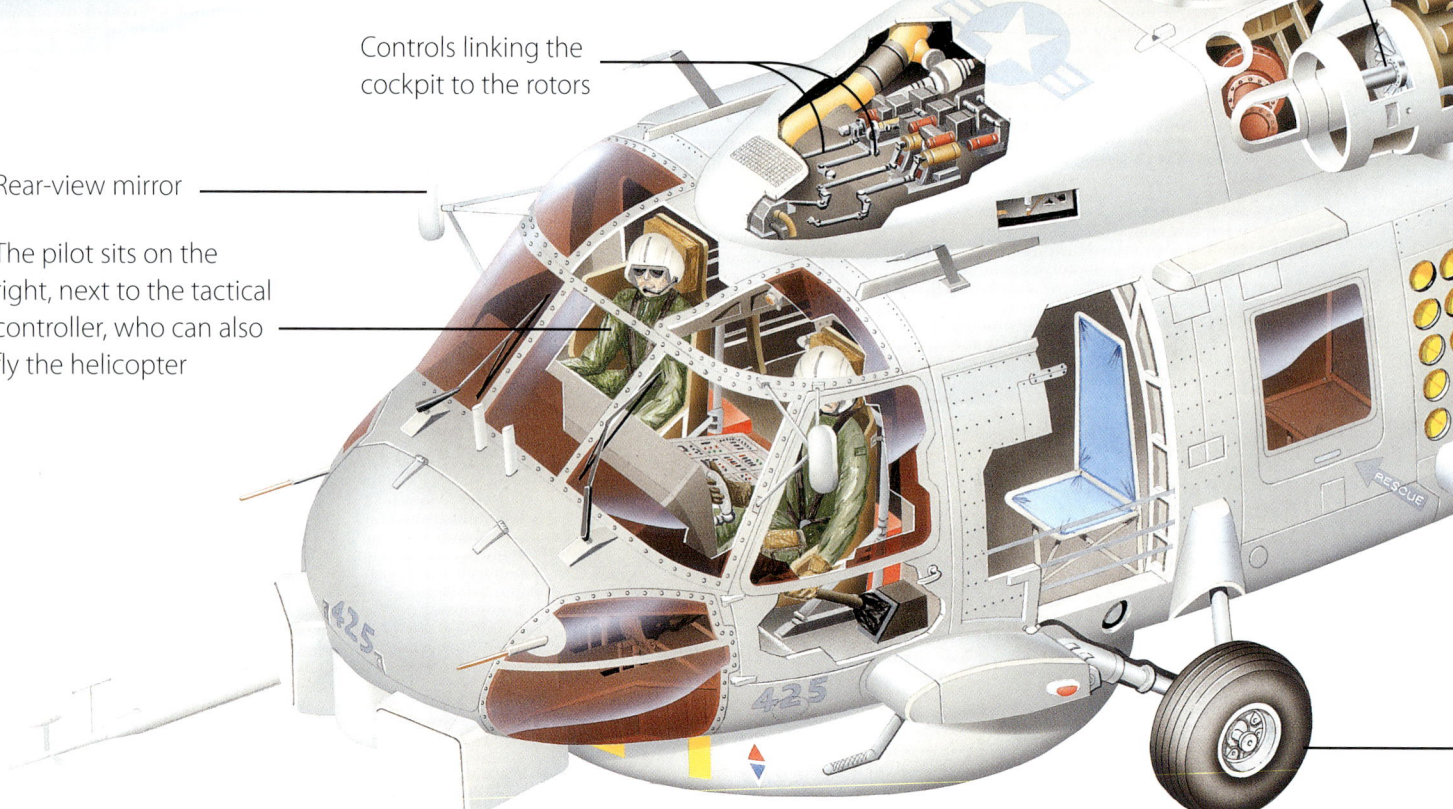

Rotor systems

The Boeing Chinook (*left, top*) has one main rotor at the front and another at the back. As they turn in opposite directions, it does not need a tail rotor. The Russian Kamov Ka-26 (*left, bottom*) has coaxial rotors. Its two rotors are mounted one above the other and rotate in opposite directions. Helicopters fitted with coaxial rotors also do not need tail rotors to stabilse them, so they are more compact than aircraft with a single main rotor.

The tail rotor pushes sideways, which stops the helicopter from spinning around

This rotating transmission shaft drives the tail rotor

The Seahawk has a large tailplane, which also helps to control the helicopter

Like an aeroplane, a helicopter's body is called the fuselage

The Seahawk's main rotor blades are made of composite material and measure 16.3 metres across

The Seahawk's sonobuoys, which contain sonar equipment, can be fired into the sea to look for submerged submarines

Landing gear – the wheels are well-sprung for landing on pitching and rolling ships' decks

DANGER KEEP AWAY

NAVY

How Rotors Work

A helicopter's rotor spins at high speed, forcing air downwards to lift the helicopter off the ground. The rotor provides not only lift, but also, when it is tilted slightly, propulsion.

   The hub of the main rotor (*see right*) is a complex mechanism that can tilt the blades at different angles to change the speed and direction of the helicopter. The pilot controls the rotor using a collective pitch lever and cyclic pitch stick. These controls raise, lower or tilt the part of the rotor called the swashplate. As the swashplate moves, it changes the pitch (angle) of the rotor blades.

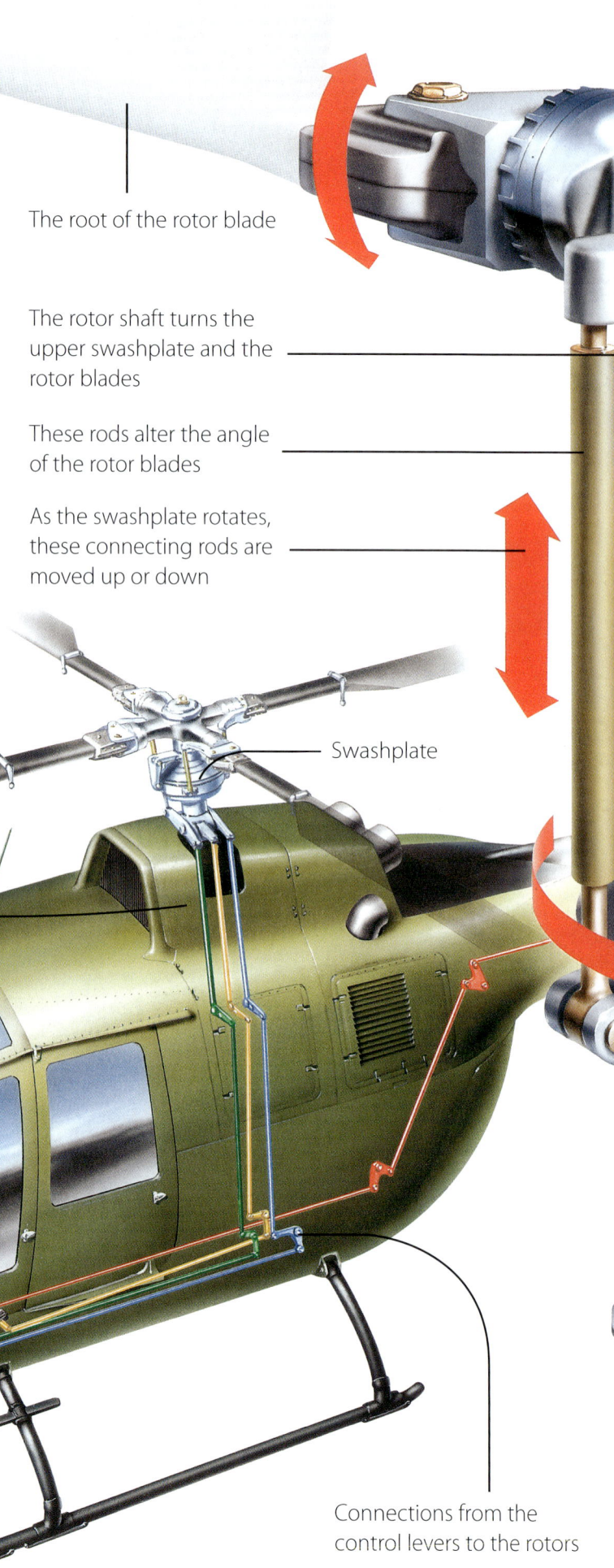

The root of the rotor blade

The rotor shaft turns the upper swashplate and the rotor blades

These rods alter the angle of the rotor blades

As the swashplate rotates, these connecting rods are moved up or down

This FH-1100 helicopter had a single turboshaft engine

Swashplate

The cyclic pitch stick controls direction of flight

These pedals control the tail rotor, which is used to steer the helicopter

The collective pitch lever controls up and down movement

Connections from the control levers to the rotors

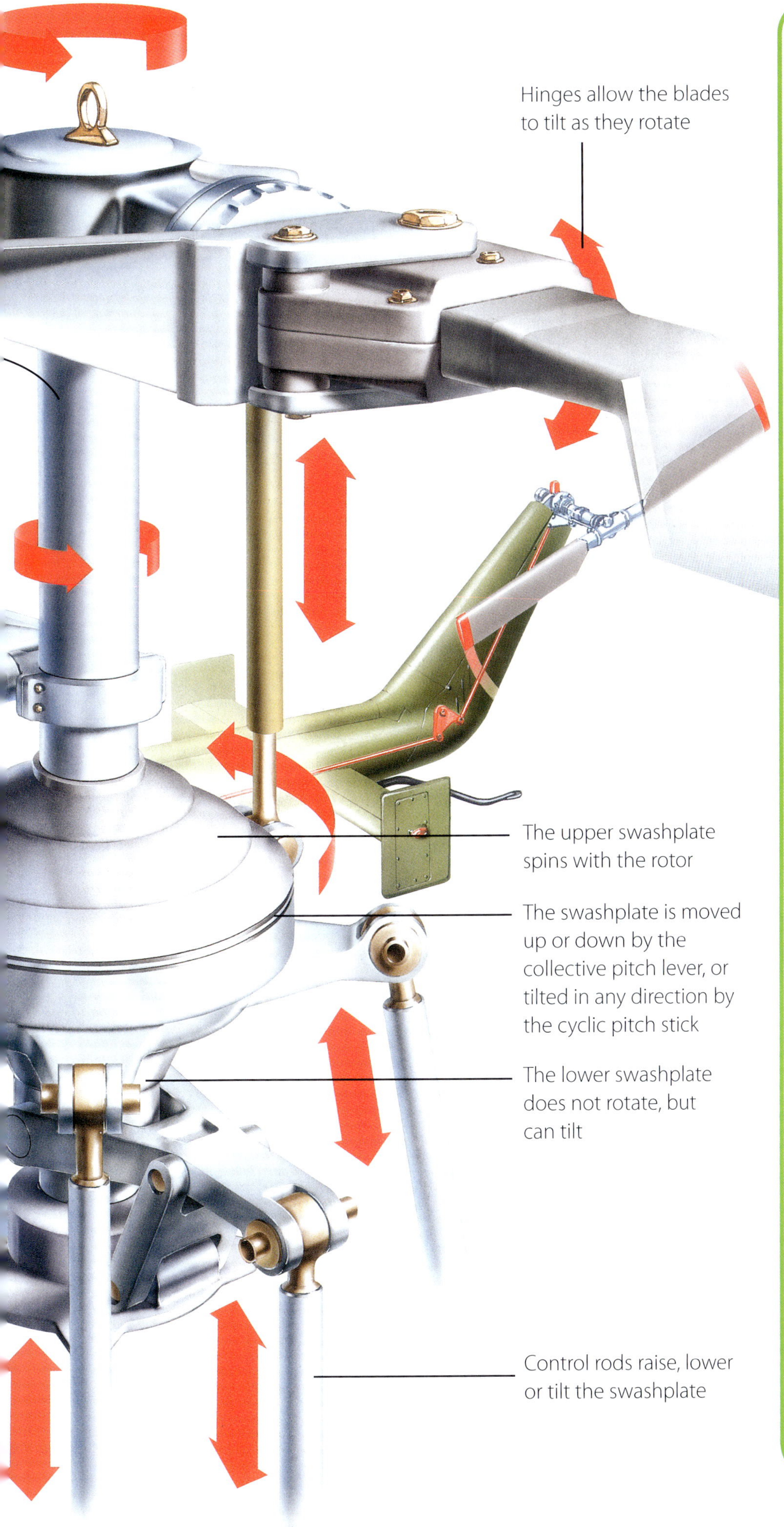

Hinges allow the blades
to tilt as they rotate

Flight control

To fly upwards, the pilot uses the
collective pitch lever to raise the
swashplate. This increases the
pitch (angle) of all the blades and
gives extra lift. To descend, the
swashplate is lowered.

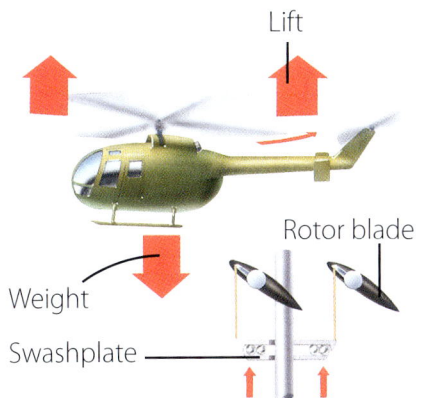

Lift

Weight

Rotor blade

Swashplate

To fly forwards, the cyclic pitch stick
is used to tilt the swashplate forward.

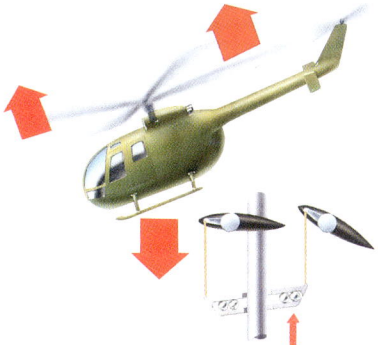

Blade pitch increases at the back
of the rotor, giving more lift from
behind, and tilts the helicopter
forwards.

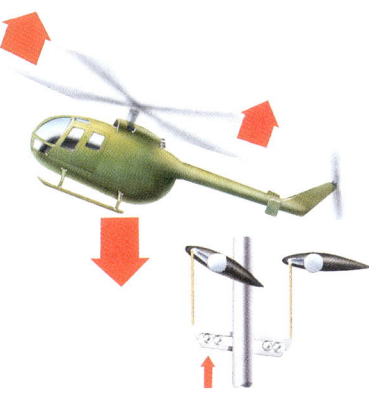

To fly backwards, the cyclic pitch
stick is pulled back. The pitch of the
blades passing the front is greater,
giving more lift at the front.

The upper swashplate
spins with the rotor

The swashplate is moved
up or down by the
collective pitch lever, or
tilted in any direction by
the cyclic pitch stick

The lower swashplate
does not rotate, but
can tilt

Control rods raise, lower
or tilt the swashplate

Index